THE THERAPEUTIC VOICE OF OLGA SILVERSTEIN

THE ART OF SYSTEMS THERAPY SERIES
Bradford P. Keeney, *Editor*

THE THERAPEUTIC VOICE OF OLGA SILVERSTEIN
Bradford P. Keeney and Olga Silverstein

THE THERAPEUTIC VOICE OF OLGA SILVERSTEIN

BRADFORD P. KEENEY
OLGA SILVERSTEIN

THE GUILFORD PRESS
NEW YORK   LONDON

To our families:

Melissa and Scott (B. K.)

Fred, Michael, Laura, Barbara, Steven, and Jeremy (O. S.)

© 1986 The Guilford Press
A Division of Guilford Publications, Inc.
200 Park Avenue South, New York, N.Y. 10003

Printed in the United States of America.

LIBRARY OF CONGRESS CATALOGING IN PUBLICATION DATA

Keeney, Bradford P.
  The therapeutic voice of Olga Silverstein.

  (The Art of systems therapy ; v. 1)
  Bibliography: p.
  Includes index.
  1. Family psychotherapy.   2. Silverstein, Olga.
I. Silverstein, Olga.   II. Title.   III. Series.
RC488.5.K443   1986   616.89'156   86-18299
ISBN 0-89862-350-2

The Art of Systems Therapy
Introduction to the Series

Bradford P. Keeney, Editor

This series connects the work of distinguished clinicians with theoretical ideas that contribute to understanding and evolving the practice of systems therapy. The title of the series, *The Art of Systems Therapy*, underscores the commitment to fostering a creative relationship between systemic ideas and clinical practice.

Each book in the series will highlight the contributions of a particular systems therapist. "Systems therapy" refers to any therapeutic orientation either explicitly or implicitly attuned to the contextual organization of human experience. These therapies encompass an incredible variety of approaches, strategies, techniques, and perspectives. The purpose of this series is to set forth the finest examples of systemically based clinical work. The series begins with this work examining the brilliant clinical style of Olga Silverstein, senior faculty member of the Ackerman Institute of Family Therapy.

The Art of Systems Therapy will provide a library of therapeutic skills and ideas for beginning and advanced practitioners. For clinical scholars and researchers, this series is a valuable resource enabling study and comparison of diverse systemic orientations to therapy. The series is dedicated to all clinicians and scholars who are committed to systemic understanding and practice of the art of psychotherapy.

B. K.

Preface

This book is a dialogue between the clinical work of Olga Silverstein and the theoretical commentary of Bradford Keeney. The collaborative effort began as a clinical research project at the Ackerman Institute for Family Therapy and evolved into a training course entitled "Patterns of Therapeutic Intervention." The clinical work and analysis that follow were part of that course.

This book is unique in that it is the study of one complete, unedited case of Olga Silverstein. We begin with a general theoretical introduction, which includes an explanation of Silverstein's clinical strategy, and then turn to clinical material to demonstrate how the theoretical map(s) provide conceptual understanding. The clinical material is interspersed with commentary as the case goes along. This enables us to structure a more dialogical format, analogous to how we have taught.

The commentary includes both a practical focus on clinical strategy and a more formal attempt to understand the process of therapy. The case is an example of Olga Silverstein's approach to systemic family therapy. By "systemic family therapy" we mean a focus on treating the patterns that connect the problem behavior of one person to the behavior of other people. Approaches to systemic therapy include the work of Watzlawick, Weakland, and Fisch (1974), Haley (1976), Selvini-Palazzoli, Cecchin, Prata, and Boscolo (1978), and Papp (1983), among others. Although Silverstein's work is rooted in these diverse traditions of systemic therapy, it clearly stands apart as a distinct clinical voice.

In the chapters that follow, we present a dialogue between practice and theory that enables one to approach an understanding of how systemic therapy may be constructed.

B. K.
O. S.

Introduction

Most therapists would agree that our own reflections and comments about what we do are at best approximate conceptualizations. Whether such conceptualizations underlie the attitudes with which we enter the therapy session or the semantic tools we later use to analyze it, they are never identical to the immediate clinical experience. Such a discrepancy between behavior and explanation is inevitable. It is operationally impossible to describe exactly what one is doing from the perspective of doing it.

In a sense, therapy is a series of largely unanticipated interactions that combine to create a communal reality between therapist and patients. In the creation of this new reality, the old reality of the family must be constantly acknowledged and accepted. Even the therapist's gradual induction of the family into a systemic mode of thinking is little more than the shaping of an identical stream of consciousness between therapist and family. Semantic utterances are at the service of such a process and undergo constant mutations. Every word triggers another word that creates a constantly shifting network of complementary perspectives. Each session holds the potential for a virtually unlimited amount of diverse opinions on the part of the therapist and patients, for there is a constant stream of mutating information coming from all sides.

A therapist may feel that a particular school of theory forms the basis of therapeutic change, but the *in vivo* emphasis must always be on selectivity and timing. This is not to say that the therapist works solely in an intuitive manner. Though it is true that years as a clinician have narrowed the gap in my work between what I'm thinking and what I'm doing, the basis of my work has always remained cognitive. During a session I am always listening intensely to the material as it streams forth from the family and looking to see how small elements of change can be inserted at the most fortuitous moment. At this point in my practice, I have reached a level where the cognitive patterns in my mind are very strongly connected. What is basically cognitive happens rapidly enough to appear almost intuitive. This does not imply, however, that there is any moment in a session when I am not trying to anticipate my next move.

A successful session is largely determined by the therapist's immediate sense of appropriateness. There are times when it is appropriate to back off, move forward, delay, reframe, repeat, or go off in another direction. Every move represents the taking of a small risk. It may produce change, or it may prove ill-timed and inappropriate. False starts have to be retracted; points of view often have to be reversed. Underneath this constant juggling act the therapist maintains an unruffled, hopefully profound point of view, based on the information injected into the system by the family. I rarely change my view about what needs to be done. All that changes is the timing.

It should be evident from such a description of clinical practice that even if there were time for lengthy theoretical reflection during the therapy process, heavily relying on it would become a disadvantage. In a sense, the pattern of interaction that grows out of each session happens as naturally as the patterns of family interaction that have brought the clients into the clinical setting. There is a pattern that flows from the interaction of the therapist and the individual family members that almost seems to create itself. The therapist merely rides the rapids of this interactional current and tries to steer the bark toward a safe and satisfactory destination.

Having someone like Brad Keeney to provide a running commentary on each step of the process is like having someone on shore, who cannot feel the rush of the current but who is perhaps in a better position to observe it. And out of this more detached observation may come a more profound, or at least a perspectively other, explanation of therapy at work.

As a performer in the process of the family's therapy, I am perhaps one of the persons least qualified to describe it fully. I am just too involved in what I am doing to remain totally aware of it. But as an observer, Brad is also absorbed by an experience: He begins to lose consciousness of himself as he becomes involved in observing. He responds immediately to the scene that he is witnessing and attempts to pin it upon the theoretical framework with which he has come equipped. In one sense, then, his position mirrors mine: He forgets himself in the observing whereas I forget myself in the acting out. Both of us have the advantages of a certain perspective, and both of our visions are limited by the peculiar boundaries of the subjective self.

A family's view of themselves, their reaction to me mediated by their expectation about therapy, my reaction to the family as filtered through the lens of my training as a family therapist, my own approach to therapy as a combination of process and content, and finally, to a certain extent, my own natural subjectivity are all elements that form the interaction witnessed by Brad. Brad's observations are in turn tempered by his theoretical approach to therapy as pure process, by his unique point of view as an observer rather than an actor, and by his own subjectivity. Then, for the reader, the experience is likely to be transformed a third time, as the transcripts of each session and Brad's commentaries come to be filtered through the lens of the reader's training, personality, and distance from the therapy situation.

The particular system of family therapy of which this book is an example had its early origins in the Brief Therapy Project at the Ackerman Institute in 1976. Two teams were involved in this project at its inception—one headed by Peggy Papp and the other by myself. The participants at that time included Richard Evans, Joel Bergman, John Clarken, Betty Lundquist, Paul De Bell, and Gillian Walker. Later we were joined by Anita Morewitz and Lynn Hoffman. Having been given the mandate to experiment, this creative group produced some interesting variations on the existing theoretical maps in the field.

By 1979 most of the team had moved on to projects of their own. The groups themselves divided, shifted, and added and lost members in an ever changing kaleidoscope of growth and reduction. The individual members remained, by and large, productive and creative.

Peggy Papp and I were left to work together as a twosome; one in the room and one behind the mirror. Many of the ideas crystalized in the work in this book were developed and integrated in that process.

It was during this period that the use of the therapeutic triangle was explored. The therapist in the room generally taking a position for change and the mysterious voice behind the mirror supporting the stability or the no-change position. Some time later we were joined by Stanley Siegel and then later by Marcia Sheinberg.

In the next phase of the project, we brought all three therapists into the room to confront the family with its own contradictions. All three positions, change, stability, and new information, were argued in the presence of the family by three therapists firmly holding the three set positions.

In 1983 I began experimenting with putting into individual practice, the concepts developed by the group.

The therapy in this book is the culmination of a gradual evolution from a single therapist with a one dimensional view of process to a multiple view divided among multiple therapists to a single therapist with a multiple view.

Such a contrapuntal process is really no different than what occurs during clinical practice, when the ideas, feelings, and words of participating individuals are woven together into a multidimensional construct that enriches and enlarges understanding. All family therapy is necessarily collaborative, and all interpretations of it should resemble the collaborative mode. Neither clinical practice nor attempts to explain its theoretical basis can ever be restricted to a single point of view.

O. S.

Contents

Theoretical Maps

This chapter presents the basic theoretical maps that will be used in analyzing Olga Silverstein's approach to systemic therapy. The first section, Domains of Observation, Description, and Intention, provides an epistemological foundation for understanding how one views therapy. In the next section, Construction of a Systemic Therapeutic Reality, we examine how a therapist and client system comes to establish and maintain a therapeutic reality. And, finally, the section called, Olga Silverstein's Strategy for Constructing Systemic Therapy unpacks Silverstein's particular approach to treatment. With these maps, the remaining chapters of the book analyze a full-length case study of Olga Silverstein.

DOMAINS OF OBSERVATION, DESCRIPTION, AND INTENTION

Since descriptions are what we have to work with when we discuss the practice and understanding of systemic therapy, we begin by distinguishing relevant differences in descriptions. One way of keeping track of differences in description is to note how descriptions are part of different domains of observing. In the context of systemic therapy, we can easily distinguish the difference between descriptions associated with observations through a one-way mirror and descriptions presented in the conversation between therapist and client.

This difference can be described as descriptions arising from the therapeutic conversation in contrast to descriptions about the therapeutic conversation. Note that the former refers more to the contributions of a *participant* in the conversation while the latter has more to do with an *observer* outside the conversation. There are times, however, when a participant can become an observer of the conversation and an observer can become a participant in the conversation. Therapists who take notice of their behavior in a session while interviewing a client system and consultants who send messages to a therapist and client system from behind a mirror exemplify these postures, respectively.

Differences in the domain of descriptions can therefore be approached by noting the differences between descriptions constructed by a participant in a conversation, by an observer of the conversation, by a participant observing his or her participation in a conversation, and by an observer participating in his or her observation of a conversation. In the context of systemic therapy we have associated these different domains with the following observational positions with respect to the therapist system:

Observational domain	*Observational position in systemic therapy*
Participant in conversation	Therapist speaking with client
Observer of conversation	Consultant or team member behind one-way mirror
Participant observing his or her participation in a conversation	Therapist noticing his or her behavior while in therapeutic situation
Observer participating in his or her observation of a conversation	Consultant sends message to therapist

In sum, the domain of observation called "participant in conversation" refers to the *view* of such a participant. The next domain, "observer of conversation," refers to the *view* of a meta-observer one step removed from the previous observer. When the participant shifts to meta-observing his or her situation or when the meta-observer shifts to more fully participating in observations, a recursion takes place. In general, the distinction "observer/observed" can be seen as recursively linked so that higher order observational domains can always be constructed.

All observers, independent of what observational domain they may be momentarily participating in, can be further seen as part of different contexts of description from within their observational domain. In a previous work (Keeney & Ross, 1985) the most fundamental distinction regarding contexts of description within any observational domain was indicated as the difference between a *semantic* and a *political* frame of reference.

A semantic frame of reference was defined as a descriptive domain primarily concerned with the construction of *meaning*. For instance, consider the following therapeutic conversation:

THERAPIST: Why have you come for therapy?
CLIENT: I hallucinate several times a day.
THERAPIST: What do you mean, exactly, by "hallucinate"?
CLIENT: You know, I hear strange voices that give me secret messages.
THERAPIST: What do you think these messages mean?

In this conversation, the therapist requests *meaning*, and the client attempts to construct it.

Later, however, the focus of the therapeutic conversation might change as follows:

THERAPIST: How often do you hallucinate?
CLIENT: At least twice a day.
THERAPIST: Who is the first person that knows you've hallucinated?
CLIENT: My wife.
THERAPIST: How does she find out?
CLIENT: I call her at work and tell her.
THERAPIST: What is the first thing she does after you tell her?

This frame of reference is not aimed at constructing meaning, but is primarily concerned with building a view of the politics of the client's situation: who-does-what-to-whom-when-and-how. Political frames of reference thus have to do with specifying the social organization of problem behavior, while semantic frames of reference specify the meaning of behavior.

Systemic therapists address different types of semantic and political frames of reference. When therapists speak of the importance of attending to (and sometimes *not* attending to) the "content" of therapy, they are usually referring to managing the wide variety of semantic frames that clients propose. With respect to semantic frames of reference, consider the following examples:

Semantic frames of reference	*Example*
Semantic frames of definition (e.g., defining the problem)	THERAPIST: What do you mean by "hallucination"?
	CLIENT: You know, I hear strange voices.
Semantic frames of explanation (e.g., explaining the problem)	THERAPIST: What do you think these messages mean?
	CLIENT: They mean that I don't know who I am.
Semantic frames about politics	THERAPIST: (*to daughter*) What do you think about the relationship between your mother and your brother?
	DAUGHTER: They're too distant from one another.

Systemic therapies have also constructed a variety of political frames of reference. These include building a view of the sequential organization of problem behavior. Such a view may be limited to discerning the sequence and relation of problem behavior and problem-solving behavior (see Watzlawick, Weakland, & Fisch, 1974), or may include a repeating social sequence in which at least three family members participate (see Haley, 1976). Other political frames of reference may indicate social coalitions (e.g., triangles and detouring) and patterns of interaction (e.g., symmetrical and complementary relations).

The relation of semantic and political frames of reference may be confused with another distinction, sometimes called "content and relationship" (see Keeney & Ross, 1985). This latter distinction refers to the dual characteristics of a single message. For instance, a client's statement, "I have hallucinations about twice a day," can be seen as describing a client's experience (content) as well as proposing that the therapist do something about it (relationship). Knowing the conversational context of this message requires looking at its broader frame of reference. If the client's statement followed a therapist's request to define why the client had come to therapy, it would be seen as arising out of a semantic frame of reference. Note what happens, however, when the client's statement is seen as arising out of the following conversation:

THERAPIST: How often do you have these hallucinations?
CLIENT: I have hallucinations about twice a day.
THERAPIST: Who else knows about these hallucinations?

This conversation indicates a political frame of reference that emphasizes the sociopolitical organization of the problem behavior rather than its meaning.

Semantic and political frames of reference, as we mentioned, contextualize the descriptions that arise from any observational domain. We, as observers of a therapeutic conversation, can note how therapy shifts between addressing semantic and political frames of reference. This view refers to how one categorizes (i.e., contextualizes) the descriptions constructed by therapist and client in the course of therapy.

Suppose that we, as observers of a particular therapeutic conversation, propose that a therapist is more joined with the wife than with the husband. Categorizing this description as a semantic or political frame of reference is a different order of categorization than framing therapist–client descriptions. Take the following example of therapeutic conversation:

THERAPIST: (*to wife*) Why does your husband continue harassing you?
WIFE: He doesn't understand me.
THERAPIST: Why doesn't he understand you?
WIFE: Because he doesn't care.
THERAPIST: (*to husband*) Why don't you care about your wife?

Since this conversation involves requests and responses about the *meaning* of husband and wife's interaction, we can say that it specifies a semantic frame of reference. An observer from behind a one-way mirror might say, however, that this conversational episode indicates the political frame, that the therapist is more joined with the wife than with the husband. If we were to ask this observer how that conclusion were reached, he or she might point out that the therapist is sitting closer to the wife and giving more eye contact to her than to the husband. In addition, the observer might say that the therapist's questions are more responsive to the wife's view and that the husband is not invited to present his own view.

These descriptions, however, are not descriptions that were constructed by the therapist, husband, or wife—they were constructed by an observer from behind a one-way mirror. The descriptions of this observer, however, can be seen as indicating a political frame of reference—but within the observational domain of the observer's descriptions of his or her observations (and not the domain of therapist and client descriptions).

Similarly, an observer of a session might inquire as to how the therapist uses affective experience to organize therapy. Although descriptions of one's own affective experience are more reliable, an outside observer is always free to make hypotheses about a client's or therapist's feelings and inner experience. Descriptions about affective experience, from whatever observational domain, may again be classified as part of a semantic or a political frame of reference. For instance, the following descriptions suggest a political frame of reference: "I get angry when she tells me to take out the trash; I then tell her she is 'queen of the naggers'; subsequently, she gets angry and then I feel hopeless." The following conversation, however, is more suggestive of a semantic frame of reference: "How do you feel about your behavior with your wife?" "It makes me depressed."

Note that these semantic and political frames pertain to the domain of descriptions constructed by clients and therapists in a session. An outside observer, as we suggested, could also make inferences about the client's (and therapist's) affective experience, such as, "The wife gets more anxious when the husband describes himself as 'depressed.'" This description of affective experience, within the domain of descriptions constructed by an outside observer, could in turn be distinguished as principally pertaining to either semantics or politics.

These examples illustrate how we can track a diversity of observational and descriptive domains involved in analyzing a therapeutic reality. We have discussed different contexts of descriptive frames of reference (in terms of semantics and politics) that are applicable to each observational domain. There is another form of analysis that can be introduced before examining how these epistemological domains lead to the construction of therapeutic realities. Given a particular observational and descriptive domain, the observer's intentions can also be distinguished with respect to whether formal understanding or practical strategy is the purpose at hand. Therapists and consultants usually shift back and forth between trying to understand a situation and trying to create a strategy for what to do with a situation. Problems may arise, however, if they talk to one another across different intentional domains. A therapist who steps outside the room to momentarily focus on formally understanding a situation may be confused and distracted by a consultant who responds by addressing the design of a therapeutic strategy (or vice versa).

As a conceptual exercise it may be useful to imagine therapists using some sort of signal system to indicate to one another which intentional domain their conversation is trying to address from moment to moment. For instance, an arrangement of different colored lights could be installed in a consultation room for conversations between supervisors and therapists. One color, say purple, would indicate that the intent of their conversation is to focus on therapeutic strategy, while a different colored light would indicate a shift to formal understanding. Of course, a third light might indicate those moments when there is an attempt to discuss the relation between formal understanding and practical strategy.

In sum, three different classes of epistemological domain have been presented:

1. Intentional domains (specified in terms of formal understanding and practical strategy).

2. Descriptive domains (specified in terms of semantic and political frames of reference).

3. Observational domains (specified in terms of observer and participant).

Each side of the distinction underlying an epistemological domain (formal understanding/practical strategy; semantics/politics; observer/participant) can also be seen as related. One's practical strategies arise out of a particular form of understanding, while one's understanding is derived from the outcomes of implemented strategies. Similarly, a sociopolitical pattern of organization (politics) leads to a particular frame of meaning (semantics) that in turn either maintains, corrects, or changes a political frame of social action. And finally, one's observing describes a way of participating and one's participation prescribes a way of observing.

As we examine systemic therapy, it will often be important to keep track of the logical typing of the descriptions we find ourselves working with. An awareness of the intentional, descriptive, and observational domains that circumscribe our descriptions provides a way of making explicit the patterns organizing how and what we know.

CONSTRUCTION OF A SYSTEMIC THERAPEUTIC REALITY

The structure of music provides a metaphorical way of talking about the construction of a therapeutic reality. In music, individual notes can be discriminated as well as heard in sequential patterns—the melodic line. Notes themselves, however, may be combined into chords, resulting in the experience of harmony and cacophony. And finally, a melodic line and its underlying harmony are coupled to give rise to repetitive themes and movements that combine into the whole system of music.

In the construction of a systemic therapeutic reality, the individual notes have to do with specific political frames of reference that spell out the sequential organization of action in a social context. These sequential patterns of organization are themselves organized by patterns of social interaction and coalition structure—in a manner analogous to the building of chords in music. These structures, in turn, are experienced and described in terms of particular semantic frames of meaning. And finally, the coupling of these political and semantic frames gives rise to repetitive themes and stories that lead to a whole therapeutic reality.

Although we may sometimes emphasize the distinction between semantic and political frames of reference, it is always possible to reinstate their connection. From this latter perspective, one cannot imagine a semantic specification of meaning as separate from a political pattern of organization and vice versa. If a logician presents a radically different paradigm for understanding the foundation of mathematics, someone (usually an accepted scientific-political authority) will build a semantic frame that suggests that the logician's work is an example of nonsense written by a madman or that it is a masterpiece created by a genius. The semantic frame giving meaning to the logician's work politically organizes the whole scientific community—the work will be published, studied, and taught or it will be ignored and possibly laughed at. Any change in the political structure prescribing meaning of the logician's work may subsequently result in shifting semantic and political frames of reference. The study of the history of science is, in effect, a study of how these changing semantic and political frames feed off one another.

In systemic therapy it is a well-known observation that semantically framing what has been previously called "problem behavior" as behavior that provides a family solution often results in a change in family politics. The subsequent political change in family organization may lead to different semantic frames that, in turn, prescribe alternative political patterns. The relation of politics and semantics is again recursive: each frame arises out of the other.

Since the political patterns are always coupled to semantic meanings, the therapist must work through meanings in order to know and influence politics. The same holds for the other perspective: knowing and influencing a client's frame of meaning requires working through his political situation. It is therefore useful to recognize that addressing any semantic frame is always a metaphorical way of getting at politics. Speaking in terms of a man's complaints about his chronic backaches may be a metaphorical way of talking about the politics of his marriage. In addition, it is useful to recognize that addressing any political frame is always a political way of getting at semantics. Reordering the sequential patterns underlying how a couple dines together may change the meaning (and politics) of their sex life.

Systemic therapy, in a nutshell, involves viewing the semantic frames presented by clients and therapist as metaphors about the politics of the problematic situation. Political frames, in turn, are viewed as coupled to systems of meaning. The art of systemic therapy involves using semantic and political frames as building blocks for the construction of alternative realities that lead to more adaptive change.[1] The therapist must begin with the semantic and political frames that clients present; these frames are the basic ingredients of the client's experiential reality. The task of therapy is to organize these same building blocks in an altered way. The desired result is that clients construct more adaptive meanings and political patterns.

---

1. "Adaptive," following Bateson (1979), refers to a better fit between a system and its environment.

The construction of an experiential reality has been previously set forth in the book *Aesthetics of Change* (Keeney, 1983). Based on Bateson's cybernetic epistemology, this perspective views experiential realities as constructed through a dialectic of process and form. More precisely, an experiential reality is constructed within the domain of description following a dialectic between descriptions of process and categorizations of form. Note that these terms are roughly analagous to political and semantic frames of reference, respectively.

Political frames thus refer to descriptions of process, usually specified in terms of simple action and interaction. The *meaning* of any simple action or interaction (semantic frame) is constructed through the naming or categorization of a political frame. The dialectical nature of this relationship between semantics and politics is such that the naming of a political frame subsequently leads one to a higher order view of political patterns.

A general map of this dialectic between semantics (classification of form) and politics (description of process) is presented in Figure 1. The right column of Figure 1, called "politics" refers to different orders of political frames. These frames arise from how an observer punctuates a sequence of action, and they are specified in the column as descriptions of simple action, interaction, and social choreography. To move from one order of political frame to another requires going through a semantic frame of meaning.[2]

Let us look at the classic "nagging husband-withdrawing wife" scenario as an example. We can begin by describing and giving meaning to simple actions. A husband's speech behavior with its accompanying body orchestration may be given the meaning of "nagging," while a wife's silence and yawning may be given the meaning of "withdrawing." At this level of analysis, the political frame of reference involves specifying behavior. Giving meaning to these behaviors recursively leads us to a higher order of analysis,

2. Some therapists advocate a neobehaviorist emphasis upon "observable facts," implying that the descriptive level of simple action is more objective and socially verifiable than other descriptive levels. This view ignores the more constructivist position that all observation is "theory-laden." The main point is that seeing "interaction" and "social choreography" shifts one's observing to higher levels than that of seeing "simple action." Learning to see these different orders of process in a way that is habitual, obvious, and socially verifiable is one of the basic tasks of becoming a systemic therapist.

ORDER OF RECURSION   SEMANTICS   POLITICS
                    (Classification of Form) (Description of Process)

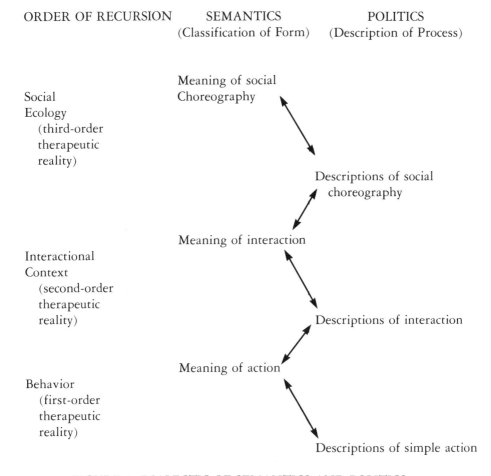

FIGURE 1. DIALECTIC OF SEMANTICS AND POLITICS

where we shift to analyzing interactional contexts. Here interaction, rather than simple action, becomes the political frame of reference. This political frame specifies an alternation between nagging and withdrawing (a description of interaction) that, in turn, may be given the meaning or classification of a "complementary relationship."[3]

3. The term "complementary relationship" is the name of a pattern of inter-action in which the actions of A and B are different but mutually fit each other (e.g., dominance-submission, exhibition-spectatorship).

This context or pattern of interaction is itself subject to a higher order of view. Social ecology—the highest order of recursion in this conceptual system—refers to how interactions are patterned as parts of a whole system of social choreography. At this level of analysis, the married couple's escalating complementary interaction may itself be subject to higher order political constraints, such as receiving a complaining call from a neighbor, the husband's having an asthmatic attack, or a child's becoming disobedient. Given this political frame, we can proceed and give it a frame of meaning. For instance, we might say that the family is caught in a "double bind."

One way of defining the goal of systemic therapy is to say it attempts to change the patterns of social choreography in a way that leads to more adaptive changes in organization (politics) and meaning (semantics). The systemic therapist, however, must utilize the client's communications as a means of building a way of knowing and influencing higher order patterns of systemic organization. For the most part, client's descriptions are on the level of descriptions of simple action and the client's associated meanings. These simple order semantic and political frames must then be transformed by the therapist into a view of interactional patterns and social choreography.

The construction of a therapeutic reality, from this perspective, entails a dialectic between semantics and politics. This dialectic leads the therapist to build a view of the patterns that connect the problem behavior of one person with the behavior of other people. With this systemic view the therapist has a perspective that is of higher logical type than that of the client, and that subsequently enables the therapist to design and implement interventions.

Systemic therapy can thus be seen as involving a series of stages, with each stage corresponding to a jump in the dialectical ladder between semantics and politics. The beginning stage involves the therapist gathering simple-order semantic and political frames. The therapist will organize information in such a way that only those building blocks that offer a way of building up a higher-order view will be emphasized and discussed. With these simple-order frames, the systemic therapist can begin moving toward the middle stage of therapy. Here the therapist attempts to build and work with a view of interactional patterns and meanings. At this stage the different actions of people are seen as related and connected. In particular, the connection of problem behavior to more encompassing patterns of interaction will be underscored. When this higher-order view is firmly established, the therapist can proceed to the final stage of systemic therapy. At this stage, diverse patterns of interaction are connected in a way that emphasizes the social choreography of a whole social ecology.

One way of looking at the construction of a systemic therapeutic reality is that most client systems come to therapy stuck in a simple-order view of their situations. Indeed, as was mentioned, most of their initial descriptions center on the politics and meanings of simple action. The therapist accepts these simple-order semantic and political frames and leads the family to higher-order realities, where their behavior is experienced as organized in a way that connects each of them as parts of a more encompassing whole system.

The above account of systemic therapy may seem to suggest that therapeutic change requires clients to achieve some form of "systemic insight." An alternative view is that it is the therapist who requires a "systemic insight" to be useful to a troubled situation. Namely, the therapist must construct a higher-order view of the situation to be able to have access to the systemic patterns organizing problem behavior. Of course, the therapist's higher-order views are always only hypotheses that heuristically suggest higher-order ways of intervening. The outcomes of a therapist's interventions, usually described in simple-order terms, help maintain, polish, and correct the therapist's ongoing hypotheses.

OLGA SILVERSTEIN'S STRATEGY FOR CONSTRUCTING SYSTEMIC THERAPY

Olga Silverstein's therapeutic strategy also involves different stages, beginning with the utilization of simple-order semantic and political frames of reference. In the beginning stage Silverstein reacts to any semantic frames the family presents as a metaphor about some political relationship in the family system. In particular, definitions of any individual's presenting problem are viewed as a semantic frame about family politics. Rather than anchoring the therapy to being centrally organized by a particular semantic frame, such as a therapeutic contract to work on a specific problem, Silverstein views all presenting semantic frames as ways the family talks about their sociopolitical patterns of organization.

Silverstein uses the presenting semantics of a family to address political frames of reference. For example, if a wife suggests that she feels like she's "inside a shell," Silverstein might respond with a political question: "With whom do you feel withdrawn?" In uncovering the coupling of semantic and political frames that specify parts of the family's system of meanings and organization, the therapist will eventually make a move toward constructing a view of patterns that connect these frames.

Silverstein's general view of the politics of family organization follows a unique political hypothesis that she developed with her colleague Peggy Papp (1983). She holds that a presenting problem is connected to each family member in a way that provides both positive and negative consequences. More specifically, the symptom or problem behavior of one individual can be seen as providing social disadvantages and advantages to each member of the family. A daughter with severe asthma not only provides a discomforting experience for herself and her mother, but may also provide a way in which they feel connected through the mother's efforts to take care of her. When the disadvantages and advantages of problem behavior are spelled out for all family members, it becomes possible to begin specifying connections between family members in terms of these positive and negative consequences (see Figure 2). A disadvantage of problem behavior for father, for instance, may be linked to an advantage for mother (or vice versa).

When a story or hypothetical explanation is constructed that enables multiple disadvantages and advantages to be tightly woven as an interlinked system, an even higher-order systemic reality is experienced. The *story that connects* then becomes the systemic therapeutic reality calibrating all subsequent communication in therapy. At this final stage, all semantic and political frames are reframed and utilized as further evidence and support of the systemic story, hypothesis, or explanation. When the therapist and family system have tightly spun this order of therapeutic reality, the family system may be dismissed from therapy. If the family were to call the therapist in the future about another problem (semantic frame), the therapist would return to the originally constructed therapeutic reality and incorporate the family's new frame within it. Seen this way, the family never really leaves therapy. The story constructed by the therapist and the family remains with them, organizing and calibrating future communications.

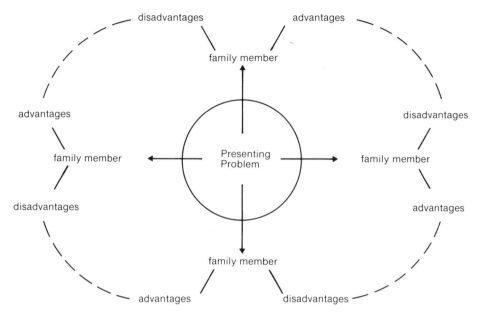

FIGURE 2. OLGA SILVERSTEIN'S GENERAL
POLITICAL HYPOTHESIS

Feedback Patterns

Another way of approaching Silverstein's therapeutic strategy involves describing the different patterns of *feedback* involved in its different stages of development. Feedback, the central idea of cybernetics, can be simply defined as utilizing the results of one's communication to help shape one's subsequent communication.

In the beginning stage of developing her systemic therapy, Silverstein constructs feedback between simple order semantic and political frames of reference. In particular, a semantic frame offered by a family member will often precipitate Silverstein to ask a question about the political frame she assumes the semantic frame is contextualizing. For instance, consider the following therapeutic conversations:

DAUGHTER: She's in outer space.

THERAPIST: How often do mother and father go out together?

DAUGHTER: Never. Well, maybe once every two months.
THERAPIST: Where are you when they go out?

In this conversation, the daughter proposes a semantic frame that the therapist hypothesizes is about the politics of Mother and Father's relationship. Daughter's response enables therapist's subsequent response to extend her focus to include daughter's own political participation.

In effect, a semantic frame introduced by a family member directs the therapist's questions about a political frame. The family's response is then used by the therapist either to scrap, to modify, or to elaborate her present line of inquiry. In this way feedback is established. This order of feedback is sketched in Figure 3.

This sketch indicates four general categories of political frame that Silverstein usually addresses in her work:

P_1 = Sequential organization of behavior
P_2 = Problem-solving behavior including involvement of referring contexts
P_3 = Social coalitions
P_4 = Past and future views of family politics

The presentation of a particular semantic frame by a family member thus directs Silverstein to address one of these classes of political frame. The family's response subsequently organizes which frame she addresses next. In this way, the beginning stage of Silverstein's therapeutic strategy involves a feedback relation between simple-order semantic and political frames.

FIGURE 3. FIRST ORDER FEEDBACK IN SILVERSTEIN'S STRATEGY

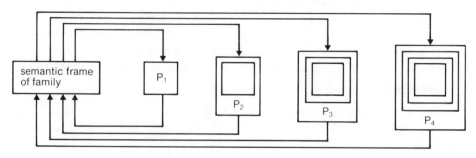

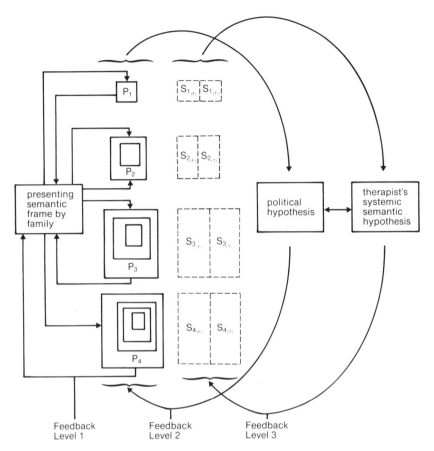

FIGURE 4. OLGA SILVERSTEIN'S THERAPEUTIC STRATEGY

The next stage of therapy moves up to a different order of feedback (see Figure 4). Here the therapist begins connecting the political information derived from the family with her hypothesis about family politics. Recall that Silverstein's political hypothesis always embodies the same underlying structure: problem behavior is connected to social advantages and disadvantages for all family members. At this stage of therapy, feedback organizes questions about family politics to help shape responses that contribute to building a view that politically connects family members.

And finally, the last stage of building her therapeutic reality involves building a systemic story, explanation, or hypothesis that embodies the family's and the therapist's semantic frames as a way of articulating the therapist's political hypothesis. The emerging story is constructed through the feedback connection between the therapist's political hypothesis and the various semantic frames that the therapist and family have previously constructed about family politics. These latter semantic frames can be seen as metaphors about "partial arcs" of family politics (see Keeney and Ross, 1985). For instance, father's problem behavior may be explained as providing a solution for a problem of mother. This view, however, is only from the perspective of one side of the relationship. We can therefore refer to this view as indicating a "partial arc" of the whole circular relationship.

In the last stage of this therapeutic approach, partial arc hypotheses become connected in a way that leads to a well-formed systemic hypothesis, that is, one that includes the participation of all relevant members of the social ecology. In the previous illustration, this might involve demonstrating how Mother's own problem behavior is complementary to Father's problem behavior and provides a solution for Father. In addition, Mother and Father's form of complementarity might be depicted as fitting into more encompassing patterns of social organization that include the behavior of their children as well as participation from other generations.

Construction of Therapeutic Interventions

We will now shift to examining how Olga Silverstein designs therapeutic interventions. In previous works (Keeney, 1983; Keeney and Ross, 1985) systemic therapeutic interventions have been depicted as addressing three general parts: stability, change, and a source of meaningful noise. The structure of a systemic intervention has been mapped as follows:

$$(\text{Stability/Change}) \; / \; \text{Meaningful Noise}$$

The left side of this expression, (Stability/Change), defines the cybernetic organization of a system: a cybernetic system achieves stability through processes of change. For instance, keeping one's balance on a high-wire (stability) requires that the acrobat constantly adjust position (change). In therapy, a troubled system can be seen as aiming to change the way it changes in order to achieve a more adaptive form of stability. Consequently, the therapist must address the complementary relation between stability and change. Efforts to singularly prescribe stability will most likely result in the troubled system demanding that its requests for change be taken seriously. On the other hand, singular prescriptions for change may result in the appearance of that beast to therapy sometimes called "resistance." Resistance, in this view, is a natural outcome from a system that has been provoked to demonstrate that its requests for stability be taken seriously.

In sum, therapeutic change can be depicted as the transformation of a system's way of achieving stability through change:

$$\text{(Stability/Change)}_1 \xrightarrow{\text{Transformation}} \text{(Stability/Change)}_2$$

To achieve such a transformation the system must encounter a source of the random or, more accurately, a source of "meaningful noise" (see Keeney, 1983; Keeney and Ross, 1985). Meaningful noise is a term that indicates not only that the system is encountering some source of the random ("noise"), but that it has some process of selection which can operate on the random (an observer who constructs "meaning"). These two components—a source of the random and a process of selection—are the ingredients of stochastic process (see Bateson, 1979). Thus, the term "meaningful noise" is a way of specifying the ingredients of stochastic process that underly all adaptive change and learning.

With this idea, a more complete specification of therapeutic change follows:

$$\text{(Stability/Change)}_1 / \text{Meaningful Noise} \rightarrow \text{(Stability/Change)}_2$$

The art of therapeutic intervention, as we mentioned before, thus requires prescribing change, stability, and a source of meaningful noise.

In Olga Silverstein's strategy the positive social consequences of problem behavior provide a rationale for prescribing stability, while the negative social consequences may be linked to prescribing change. Meaningful noise refers to how the therapist lays out an explanation for prescribing these complementary sides. The most common sources of meaningful noise may be constructed from family history, cultural myth, psychobabble, religious metaphor, stories about other clients (fictional or not), and so forth. The semantic frames clients propose or request usually provide a clue to what form of noise will be meaningful. A student of Eastern thought might be given a reading from the *I Ching*, whereas a deacon of a Baptist Church may require some obscure biblical reference. A client who happens to be a family therapist, however, may have to be given a theoretical mythology, such as Ericksonese or Satirese.

Olga Silverstein's strategy involves prescribing various ways of addressing stability, change, and meaningful noise in therapy. In the beginning of therapy, the client's presenting semantic frame may be stabilized (often through accepting the client's choice of metaphor), while a change in the politics it is assumed to be about may be implied. The source of meaningful noise involves drawing upon the semantic frames the clients have already presented. Consider the following therapeutic conversation:

MOTHER: (*referring to husband*) I've stopped being a mother to him.

THERAPIST: You think you changed from being a sort of "good mommy" to him to an "angry mommy"? Is that where it's gone?

Here the therapist addresses *stability* through emphasizing that mother is still a "mommy" to her husband, but introduces *change* by speaking about how her way of "mommying" has changed. Her choice of terms for describing this change—"good mommy" to "angry mommy"—provides a source of *meaningful noise*.

As therapy progresses, stability can more readily refer to underscoring how problem behavior provides a positive contribution to stabilizing and maintaining a relationship, while change can address the negative consequences that arise from the particular way stability is being maintained. Meaningful noise now involves making semantic references to higher-order political frames that further hint at a social organizational view of how problem behaviors link people together. Consider the following therapeutic conversation:

WIFE: Why should he continue staying out all night?

THERAPIST: It keeps your mind off worrying what to do with your parents [stability]?

WIFE: But he's driving me crazy!

THERAPIST: The two of you do pay a price [change implied] for the way you've chosen to be loyal to your parents [meaningful noise].

Stability addresses how problem behavior, in this case the husband's staying out all night, contributes to stabilizing the wife's relationship with her parents. Change is subsequently implied when the therapist acknowledges the price (in terms of negative consequences) their solution requires. And, finally, meaningful noise points to how their relationship contributes and fits as part of a more encompassing family ecology.

Silverstein's therapy culminates in the creation and maintenance of a well-formed systemic story or explanation about the family's situation. At this stage, all semantic and political frames the family has presented will be recycled and incorporated into the therapist's systemic explanation. Her explanation, embodying the political hypothesis that connects problem behavior to social disadvantages and advantages, provides the way in which stability and change become more fully addressed. At this stage, the therapist speaks more and more about the family's "dilemma." Since problem behavior provides social advantages, its contribution to stability must be addressed. However, at the same time, the social disadvantages of the problem suggest that change is necessary. The therapist at this stage often repeats her explanation of the family's dilemma, each time adding to it the additional semantic and political frames the family offers.

In conclusion, Silverstein's strategy demonstrates how a dialectic between semantics and politics constructs a systemic therapeutic reality. The context of this dialectic is a conversation between therapist and clients. As Szasz has suggested, psychotherapy is not to be understood in terms of medical interventions, but in terms of the structure of rhetoric. The systemic therapy of Olga Silverstein fully utilizes the rhetorical structure of therapy and builds upon the understanding that therapy is primarily within the epistemological domain of description.

In systemic therapy, what emerges are stories and stories about stories. Stories reveal how people construct their world and therefore provide clues for knowing their epistemological premises. In general, therapy is a process of weaving stories between therapist and client systems. Attending to symptomatic communication is one way of hearing a story. To paraphrase Bateson, the therapist must be shrunk to fit the procrustean bed of the client's stories. The therapist then builds her own story in response to the one she has been told. From a cybernetic perspective, when an exchange of stories is structured in terms of feedback, self-correction and adaptive change become possible.

The stories people live as well as their stories about those stories are all a therapist has to work with. In this sense, therapy is indeed a conversation, an exchange of stories. As Szasz (1978, p. 11) summarizes, "Seeing therapy as conversation rather than cure thus requires that we not only consider the error of classifying it as a medical intervention, but that we must also look anew at the subject of rhetoric and assess its relevance to mental healing."

It should be no surprise that poets are well aware of these concerns. Gary Snyder (1979, p. 29), for instance, describes poetry as "a hook; a net to trap, to clutch, and present; a sharp edge; a medicine, or the little awl that unties knots." This provides a tidy metaphor for systemic therapy, where knots of description are embodied in the stories clients and therapists construct. In the chapters that follow, it will be clear how Olga Silverstein's systemic therapy, like poetry, attempts to untie these knots.

SESSION ONE

Therapeutic Building Blocks

As part of a clinical training course, Olga Silverstein sought a family for treatment. She selected a family that had called the Ackerman Institute for Family Therapy requesting help. The intake sheet read as follows:

> William and Lily Thomas both suffer from depression which has an adverse effect on their marriage and is affecting their children. William says that he becomes introverted and "goes into himself." He is an alcoholic—went on a month-long drinking binge a few months ago. He can't seem to hold a job. Tommy (the older son) is "hard to reach"; hates his father, is "becoming harder and harder to reach." The younger boy was described as distracted and anxious.

With this information Olga Silverstein called the family's home, spoke to Mr. Thomas, and set a date for the following week. The family did not show. Subsequently, Silverstein called Mr. Thomas and set a new appointment date. No critical comments were given.

All family sessions were observed by a group of clinicians. In addition, all sessions (a total of four) were videotaped. What follows is a transcription of these sessions with commentary. The family, a middle-class black family, consisted of mother, father, and two sons, Tommy and Benji.

THERAPIST: Okay. Now because of the time—
FATHER: Yeah.
THERAPIST: We have only till seven o'clock tonight—
FATHER: That's okay.
THERAPIST: —so it's going to be a little short. Hmm. What's your name?
OLDER SON: Tommy.
THERAPIST: Tommy. And the little guy?
YOUNGER SON: Benji Michael.
THERAPIST: Hmm?
YOUNGER SON: Benji Michael.

THERAPIST: What's your first name? Benji?

YOUNGER SON: Benji Michael.

THERAPIST: Benji. Tommy and Benji. Mr. Thomas, Mrs. Thomas. Okay. I'm Mrs. Silverstein.

Comments: Some observers of this session might propose that the therapist's use of "Mr." and "Mrs." is a political action marking a generational boundary. Note, however, that this political frame refers to the observational domain of the observer's own descriptions and not the descriptions of the family and therapist. In other words, there has been no literal discussion of generational boundaries in this session, although an outside observer could construct such a description and then note that he or she has constructed a frame about family politics.

MOTHER: Hi.

THERAPIST: Okay. Now I don't know if the lady you spoke to explained to you about the mirror.

FATHER: Yes, she did.

MOTHER: Well, I didn't speak to her, my husband did.

THERAPIST: You did.

FATHER: Yeah, I did.

THERAPIST: So you know that this is a one-way mirror and there are some people behind the screen? That's a video camera up there—

FATHER: Um-hum.

THERAPIST: Okay.

MOTHER: What is the video camera used for?

THERAPIST: Hmm?

MOTHER: What is the video camera used for?

THERAPIST: I'll tell you. We take a tape of the session and then we study it, we look at it, sometimes used for teaching. I need your signature, both of you, on it.

FATHER: Okay.

THERAPIST: Okay. How old are you, Tommy?

TOMMY: Fifteen.

THERAPIST: Fifteen. And Benji, how old are you?

BENJI: Seven.

THERAPIST: Seven. My, you're a big boy. Is it still snowing out?

MOTHER: Unzip your coat, Benji.

Comments: An observer might claim that the mother tends to take an oppositional position with the therapist. Recall the exchange where the therapist asked the family if the one-way mirror setup had been explained. The father said he knew that and the mother immediately qualified his response by saying that she hadn't spoken to anyone. That exchange, in light of the present one where the therapist suggests that Benji is a "big boy," followed by mother's command for Benji to unzip his coat (treating him like a "little boy"), could be seen as indicating an oppositional position. Such a view might further lead an observer to hypothesize that the therapist and the father are more joined than the therapist and the mother, planting the seeds for a possible coalition. All of these frames of reference pointing to family politics are again from the domain of an observer's descriptions and not from the domain of description arising within the session. (For the rest of this case, we will emphasize the descriptions that arise out of the therapeutic session, rather than the descriptions an observer could construct about it.)

THERAPIST: Okay. So since we have such a short time let me ask you what brings you here.

Comments: The therapist, in asking "what brings you here" requests that the family provide her with an account of what specifically happened to lead them to seek a therapist's help.

FATHER: Well, just family problems which stem from—basically my drinking caused the problem with the family.

Comments: This response does not specify what particular event or sequence of events occurred that led to the family's decision to call a therapist. The father's response only provides a general "semantic frame of reference" that defines the meaning of their presence in therapy as having something to do with "family problems" and "his drinking."

THERAPIST: Are you drinking now?

Comments: Rather than pursue a more elaborate specification of the semantic frame of reference suggested by the father, the therapist turns to requesting specific information about father's present drinking behavior.

FATHER: No. Not really. And—
THERAPIST: He is? Yeah?
FATHER: Uh-huh.
THERAPIST: Benji says yes.
FATHER: Benji says yes, it must be yes.
THERAPIST: Must be yes, right?
FATHER: So it caused a lot of hostilities and depressions and—and varied and different effects on the family.

Comments: The father moves away from providing specific information about his present drinking behavior and shifts back to a semantic frame of reference that further suggests the meaning of what has happened. With this move, we can already see a basic communication pattern in this therapy. Namely, two communicational frames of reference have been introduced. The first, what we have called a "semantic frame of reference," underscores the construction of meaning. The second, what we have called a "political frame of reference" in the previous chapter, focuses on the social organizational aspects of communication that specify "who-does-what-to-whom-when."

As we watch this therapy we will note how these two frames of reference constantly shift back and forth. When the therapist began by asking "What brings you here?" a political frame was actually requested—that is, information that would point to the specifics of who had done what to whom at what time that led them to seek therapy. The father, however, responded with a semantic frame by suggesting the general notions of "family problems" and "his drinking." Subsequently, the therapist asked a political question about his drinking—"Are you drinking now?" Following a mixed response, father again returned to semantics ("it caused a lot of hostilities and depressions"). We will continue to depict this therapy as how therapist and family manage the organization of these semantic and political frames of reference.

THERAPIST: Oh, yes.
FATHER: And—well, it's not just—it's an accumulation of problems. It's just not the—
THERAPIST: It's not just drinking.
FATHER: And I just came to a point where something had to be done before I lost everything, so I got in touch with somebody

through the public school system and they told me I should stop by here, so I'm here now.

> *Comments:* When the therapist joined with father's semantic frame ("it's not just drinking"), the father responded with a political frame indicating that the public school personnel are involved in helping him solve the problem. At this point, the therapist's questioning of the father has uncovered two political frames of reference: (1) information about his present drinking behavior (he's now drinking), and (2) someone in the public school system has been involved in trying to solve the problem. In terms of semantic frames of reference, the father has addressed two classes of semantic frames: (1) the semantic frame of defining the problem—"family problems" and "his drinking"; and (2) the semantic frame of explaining the problem.
>
> These semantic and political frames of reference that the father has presented in response to the therapist's questioning may be seen as potential building blocks for constructing a therapeutic reality. Throughout this session, the therapist will continue participating in the family's construction of these communicational frames. Note that her participation involves first-order feedback, where a family semantic frame is usually addressed in terms of its underlying politics. The family's subsequent response, in turn, helps shape which semantic or political frame the therapist will next address. In this way, the ingredients for constructing a useful (and "therapeutic") reality for the family is created.

THERAPIST: I see. Okay. Would you agree, Mrs. Thomas, that that's the major problem—is his drinking?

> Comments: The therapist's question, on one level, is a return to father's initial semantic frame—"his drinking." On another level, asking whether the mother agrees with her husband's choice of semantics is one way of searching for a political difference or connection between them.

MOTHER: Yeah. I would say that and plus that branches off from other problems.
THERAPIST: Um-hum. Like—could you be a little more specific?

Comments: The therapist requests additional semantics.

MOTHER: Let me see. Yes, his drinking is his main problem, but I believe his drinking is symptomatic of another problem that he has.

THERAPIST: That *he* has.

Comments: The therapist underscores the political implication of her semantic response.

MOTHER: Yes. So, therefore, his drinking has caused the rest of the family to have problems.

Comments: This is the same semantic frame of explanation that father initially introduced.

THERAPIST: Aha. Okay. What other problems in the rest of the family?

Comments: A request for other semantic frames that define problems.

MOTHER: Well, personally speaking, with me I am—I'm not as warm and attentive to my children as I should be, because I'm affected by alcoholism. Has put me in somewhat of a—not a shell, but somewhat of a shell.

Comments: Note that the response, "I'm not as warm and attentive to my children as I should be" is a semantic frame that indicates a problem in family politics—mother's relationship with her children.

THERAPIST: So you've kind of withdrawn from your husband—

Comments: The therapist recycles the wife's semantic frame of "put me in . . . a shell" by articulating it as a semantic frame about the political relationship between husband and wife ("you've kind of withdrawn from your husband"). If the wife accepts this semantic frame about politics, then the therapist can directly address its political side. For instance, she might then ask, "when did you first notice that you'd withdrawn from him?," or, "who in the family is the least withdrawn from your husband?," or such.

MOTHER: Well, I'm not worried about my husband, so much, anymore. I'm worried about my children.

Comments: Wife's response negates possibility of using therapist's previous semantic frame about politics. Therapist will accordingly shift to constructing a different semantic frame about politics—depicting the wife as "withdrawn from the family."

THERAPIST: Withdrawn from the family.

MOTHER: Um-hum. It's causing conflict within the household. My youngest son is anxious now, and I think it's because of emotional problems in the house.

Comments: Wife again negates possibility of exploring therapist's semantic frame about politics and offers a new semantic frame that defines another problem: son's "anxious" behavior. The therapist will now zoom in to ask a political question about this semantic frame. Note that the previous sequence of questions with the mother can be seen as attempts by the therapist to utilize the mother's semantic frames in a way that will lead to exposing political patterns—first-order feedback (see previous chapter).

THERAPIST: Anxious by the school's report or by what you see?

FATHER: School's report—

MOTHER: By what I see also, because I know my own child better than the teacher does—

THERAPIST: Yeah, of course—

MOTHER: —so, in spite—first—

THERAPIST: And you see him as being what—anxious? Um-hum. What have you tried to do about the drinking problem?

Comments: Having widened the therapeutic focus (semantic frames defining problems) to include the wife's withdrawn behavior and the son's anxious behavior, the therapist returns to asking political information about what the wife has done about the husband's drinking. The wife responds with political information about previous problem-solving efforts.

MOTHER: I've been through this with him for a long time. I've been to Alanon—

THERAPIST: Oh, you have.

MOTHER: He's been to A.A. I went back—I only went to Alanon twice because I didn't—didn't particularly care for their concept, so—I didn't feel that it didn't do anything for me. I've been in therapy myself—individual therapy. He stopped drinking for five years or four years, but that doesn't matter, now that he's drinking again—

THERAPIST: I see.

MOTHER: —and it's progressive. And I feel that —um—he's worse off than he was six, seven years ago.

THERAPIST: You stopped for four, five years, with the help of A.A.?

Comments: The therapist asks the husband for political information about his drinking.

FATHER: On my own.

THERAPIST: On your own. And started again how long ago?

FATHER: Well, the last two years on and off.

THERAPIST: Oh, last two years. Are you working?

Comments: Recall that one aspect of Olga Silverstein's strategy for systemic family therapy involves looking for how the presenting problem(s) can be seen in terms of positive and negative social consequences. Seen this way, problems provide a dilemma—there is as much reason to maintain them for their positive social consequences as there is reason to alleviate them. When the therapist asks about the husband's work, she may find information that reveals some possible social consequences of his drinking.

FATHER: Um-hum.

THERAPIST: What do you do?

FATHER: Sanitation worker.

THERAPIST: Are you able to work and keep your job? Does that interfere with your —

FATHER: Not at all. Not at all. It doesn't — the only thing it int—it doesn't inter—it just—my—my family, you know? I am—

THERAPIST: Your're able to maintain your job —yourself on a job?

FATHER: I'm able to maintain my job, but I have problems

with my bills, I fall behind. I just don't seem to be able to put it all together, you dig? It's not the cash flow. The cash flow is positive but I always end up in the red, all the time. It just seems to be one big problem. It's just getting worse and worse.

Comments: The father shifts frame of reference to semantics involving problems with paying his bills.

THERAPIST: Um-hum. Now, you see any other—anything else other than the drinking or—in those four—let me put it differently, in those four, five years when—what's your first name?
FATHER: Tommy.
THERAPIST: You're also William, senior. Do you mind if I call you William?

Comments: Some observers might note that the therapist is using semantics to suggest a political change. Specifically, calling the father "William, senior" rather than "Tommy" more clearly recognizes his role as an adult in this family.

FATHER: No, of course not, of course not.
THERAPIST: And your first name?
MOTHER Lily.
THERAPIST: Lily, Okay. That would—Lily, while he was not drinking, how did things go?

Comments: The therapist is again exploring the social consequences of the husband's drinking.

MOTHER: He's always been inconsistent. Umm—I think it comes—it stems from the way he was raised. He was raised with older people. His father was an alcoholic. His mother left him when he was a very young child so his grandmother—as I said, he was raised by older people and they always died off on him, so I think from that he's very cold. I guess somewhere in his young childhood he turned off his emotions, thinking that everybody would desert him after a while, because of the death. Umm—and—he's a dreamer and sometimes he has a problem—a lot of the times he has a problem separating the reality from the dream, where he will neglect priorities to go after a dream that's irresponsible.

Comments: The mother offers semantic frames that attempt to explain her husband's drinking. Also note that the mother calls her husband a "dreamer." As we will later see, this is a clue for building the foundational theme of "high expectations" in session two.

THERAPIST: Um—hum, can you give me an example?

Comments: This request for a particular example is a way of steering the communication toward political information.

MOTHER: Why don't you give her the example—examples, plural.

FATHER: I can give her an example. I quit my job and I went into the construction business, which I knew nothing about. I just had a whole lot of enthusiasm, some friends that I knew from childhood who made it quite easy for me to think that I could do that. I just—what I did was irresponsible. I mean—I can say —

THERAPIST: Um-hum. How long ago was that?

FATHER: This—this was—this was about two years ago and then some people came back to me about a year—about eight months ago to do a project for them and I got involved in construction again and it didn't turn out—same way—it's just—you can't pay bills with promises, and all the good intentions in the world, that's great, but when it came down to the bottom line the individual didn't have the cash he intended to, or he said he did, so another goose chase. I was stuck out on a limb and promises made that were never kept and my son, I promised to take him to the game, football game and—15 years of promise and he's fed up with it, which I don't actually blame him for.

THERAPIST: Um-hum. You accept the notion that you're the problem, that you're the chief problem in the family. Hmm?

Comments: The therapist contextualizes (i.e., semanticizes) the father's descriptions of his past failures as possibly meaning that he is the "chief problem in the family" (a semantic frame about family politics).

FATHER: Definitely, definitely. I just want to know what to do about it. I know—my problem stems—

Comments: The father accepts this generalized semantic frame and requests political information—what to do about it.

THERAPIST: Well actually your wife has some—you know— Lily has some pretty—seems to have a great deal of empathy, sympathy, or understanding that you had a hard life growing up and things were rough and that's what—what's your idea about what this is all about?

> *Comments:* The therapist sidesteps politics and points to semantics regarding what his problem means. She points to the semantic frames of explanation his wife has provided and then asks him to construct some further semantic frames.

FATHER: It's like—I tell you—I'll explain it the best way I know how. I've never been totally happy. I never had—my highs—my highs—I never peak on anything. Oh, I peak every now and then when I think I'm getting involved in something, I peak very much and then lull out so I'm very—I appear on the exterior to be a very pleasant, happy person, but inside I am not so—I never was, I never could remember a time when I could say I was happy, so something—and that's why—the drinking situation is a symptom. If I can stop drinking for five years and I can stop drinking for eight months and I can stop drinking for six months, obviously I can get a hold on it, but I keep going back because something inside, I haven't settled. What, I don't know. I feel if I can get a handle on what's causing this whole paranoiac episode of mine or whatever you want to call it I'd feel a lot better about this.

> *Comments:* The father provides further semantic frames of explanation. Note that mother's and father's explanations of his drinking involve two general notions: (1) it's related to his family of origin, and (2) "something inside [him] isn't settled." In the previous chapter, the process of therapeutic change was depicted as requiring some source of the random out of which new patterns may be constructed—what was called "meaningful noise." The most obvious source of meaningful noise for troubled clients arises out of their own hunches and hypotheses about their problematic situation. The job of the therapist is to manage such information in a way that enables the clients to utilize it as a therapeutic resource. In this case, family history and the idea that the father needs to settle an issue are emerging as possible sources of "meaningful noise."

THERAPIST: Um-hum. (*To son*) Tommy, let me ask you, your're kind of an observer in the scene these days. What do you think is going on here?

Comments: The therapist asks the son for semantics about family politics.

TOMMY: Well, this—kind of family problems, but what's concerning me is my father. Well, when I was younger I didn't depend on my mother as I would now. I depended—because she was a woman and I didn't know how to go to a mother. I'd go looking for my father. If I had a problem I would go to my father—

Comments: This indicates that Tommy may presently be in a coalition with his mother against his father.

THERAPIST: Aha, you go to him, uh-hum.

TOMMY: —cause I couldn't understand how I could go to my mother because she was a female so I went—I'd try to go to my father—he was never there. Anything I needed he was never there.

THERAPIST: So then what would you do?

TOMMY: So over the years I've learned how to do things for myself. I asked him to show me how to play sports; he's never there to help me out with that so I learned how to do it by myself and now I'm very good at it. So—

THERAPIST: So you're a pretty independent fellow, generally?

TOMMY: Yes. He's—I kind of blocked him out now—that I don't need a father. I don't need him anymore.

Comments: The son's responses are semantic frames about politics: When he needed his father, his father wouldn't be available; therefore he learned to do things on his own. In addition, his mother, in his view, cannot provide him with the resources his dad, as a male, can offer.

THERAPIST: You're also angry at him. Hmm?

Comments: The therapist offers a new semantic frame: the son is angry at his father.

TOMMY: Not really angry. Yeah, kind of—just let down.

Comments: The son responds with an alternative semantic frame about his relationship with his father: feeling "let down."

THERAPIST: You feel let down.

TOMMY: Yeah. And I don't feel like showing no more feelings, cause I gave him a lot now. I just can't take all these letdowns.

Comments: Here is another semantic frame possibly defining a problem—Tommy can't take those letdowns.

THERAPIST: Um-hum. In the arguments between your mom and dad, are you generally on her side or no side or what?

Comments: The therapist seeks political information that may expose social coalition patterns.

TOMMY: I don't get on either side. I'm right in the middle all the time. I stay in-between.

Comments: This is a semantic frame about the triadic political relations of son, mother, and father: the son is in the middle of their arguments.

THERAPIST: You stay in-between. Um-hum. Are you the peacemaker in the family? If they fight or argue do you try to keep things quiet or—
TOMMY: I just try to ignore—you know—block it out.

Comments: Political information that further suggests that the son is in-between his father and mother—he ignores them in some unspecified way.

THERAPIST: How about Benji, what do you see, does he get involved in their stuff?

Comments: This is a request for political information that may expose how Benji is involved in sequences of interaction embodying parental arguments.

TOMMY: He comes to me.
THERAPIST: Oh, he comes to you.
TOMMY: He says. "Why are they fighting?" and I tell him, "Well, they're going to fight sometimes so don't worry about it." I take him outside so he can forget about it, so he don't have to be around it. Cause if he's around it, he gets very upset.
THERAPIST: Then you kind of take care of him and—

Comments: The therapist semanticizes this political frame by saying that Tommy "take[s] care" of his younger brother, Benji. When Tommy accepts this semantic frame, the therapist will add the additional semantic frame that he is a "pretty good kid" which, in turn, enables the therapist to point out that the parents must have done "something right"—a semantic frame about political relations of parents to children.

TOMMY: Yeah. Try to keep him out of the room or blast the radio or something so he can't hear it.

THERAPIST: (to mother) Um-hum. Um-hum. So you've got a pretty good kid here.

MOTHER: Um-hum.

THERAPIST: Must have done something right.

MOTHER: I think I've done something right when I raised him, 'cause I feel that I raised him by myself with no help from my husband at all, and the only help I did get from him was when I had my second child, but it wasn't really help because he was doing everything else wrong financially. You know—just messing up. Promises—promises, promises. Not fulfilling what he set out to do. Never finishing anything, never any consistency. You know—always putting me down, always hollering and screaming at the kids and it was always the point where he had to be the focal point of attention in the household, where he was the baby, and I always felt like—you know—like we had to walk around him. That he was the one being raised when actually these two are the ones being raised.

Comments: The mother offers semantic frames about the political relations of parents to children and in particular suggests that her husband was like a third "baby" in the family. The therapist will politically address that semantic frame.

THERAPIST: (to father) Benji is on your side, though.

FATHER: Um-hum.

Comments: One could hypothesize that mother and Tommy are joined against father, while father and Benji are joined against mother.

THERAPIST: Was there a time when you did baby him?

MOTHER: My husband?

THERAPIST: Um-hum.

Comments: This is a turning point in the session. The theme of "mothering" provides a semantic way of discussing family politics, particularly mother and father's relationship. Note that this theme was introduced by the family: the therapist recycles it in a way that more specifically addresses political patterns of organization.

This stage of systemic family therapy may now be seen as how a therapist manages semantic frames in a way that provides access to reorganizing family politics. The family provides the semantics which the therapist recycles in feedback fashion. How the therapist works with these semantic frames determines the way in which family politics get addressed.

When a therapist wants a semantic frame about a particular political relationship, she may invent one and present it to a family member who will then accept it, modify it, or offer an alternative frame. For instance, when Silverstein suggested earlier that the older son was "angry" with his father, he rejected that frame and offered the notion that he was "let down." The therapist, in this case, was therefore successful in getting a semantic frame to talk about father and son's relationship. Whether the son is *really* "angry" or "let down" is irrelevant to the therapist. What is important is that both the therapist and the boy have found a semantic frame (or "metaphor") that enables them to talk about his relationship with his father. In general, the therapist will continue to hunt for semantic frames that are about relationship and social ecology rather than individual dynamics.

MOTHER: Oh, sure. It's —it's just been the past three to four years that I stopped babying him and started realizing that I had my own children that needed me and needed to be babied, and plus my mother—my mother helped me out a lot also by saying things that— I guess it was very obvious that I was neglecting my children and—

Comments: Discussion of the semantic frame of mother "babying" her husband introduces another political member: grandmother.

THERAPIST: —babying him.
MOTHER: —babying him and focusing on him.
THERAPIST: I was going to ask you if there was a grandma here, who—

Comments: The therapist addresses grandmother's participation in family politics.

MOTHER: Well, she is in—she is in Georgia, though.

THERAPIST: Since—she's been in Georgia all along or—she's not been—

MOTHER: Well, she's been there now for about nine years. Eight or nine years.

THERAPIST: Eight or nine years, so he was quite a little fella then and—she moved to Georgia. Before that was she very active in your household and in—

MOTHER: Yeah, yeah,—uh—yeah.

FATHER: I'd say she was. Very positive note.

MOTHER: But she always minded her—

THERAPIST: Very positive? With you too?

MOTHER: She always minded her business.

FATHER: Um-hum. Yeah. She was—I never had any problem with my in-laws that I didn't create myself. Let's put it that way.

Comments: These semantic frames about grandmother's political involvement in family life indicate that she was possibly joined more closely with mother and had some conflict with father.

THERAPIST: You're feeling pretty down on yourself these days.

FATHER: It's a reality. I'm willing to face up to it for once. I created a mess that I wanted desperately to get out of, and I wouldn't be able to achieve any success unless I admit exactly what I've done and try—try to right it.

Comments: The father provides semantics about the problematic situation. The therapist will now utilize these semantic frames to address present political relations between the husband and wife.

THERAPIST: Um-hum. (*To mother*) You don't—you have no faith in that.

MOTHER: No. Because he's broken too many promises—

THERAPIST: It seems like you've heard that one before.

MOTHER: —because he's broken too many promises and he's told lies to me and I've been totally a good woman to him and he couldn't have gotten it—it's getting to the point—it was getting to the point where I could put a halo on my head and call myself Saint

Lily, but there is not any saints on earth. The only saints are in heaven, if there is any and that's not normal, that's abnormal. I mean for you to deny yourself everything and—and—and have your whole world revolve around someone else and I started realizing that something must be wrong with me. I must not have good self-esteem and I didn't, because he was robbing it from me and I let him. I allowed him to do it and now since—since I've been in therapy I've—

Comments: The mother provides semantic frames that begin to define her problems. The therapist will now address the only statement in mother's response that relates to politics—her involvement in therapy.

THERAPIST: So what happened—oh, you've been in therapy.
MOTHER: Yeah. I should have never stopped therapy. I went into therapy right after I had my second child because I had very bad blues after I had Benji and I went into therapy for about—I guess about eight months. It was six months, seven months?

Comments: At this point, a problem has been defined for every family member—father's drinking, Benji's anxiety, Tommy's inability to show feelings and problem with being let down by father, and now, mother's difficulties with her self-esteem (and possible depression).

FATHER: About six months.
MOTHER: Six months.
THERAPIST: And therapy helped you somehow to think more—taking care of yourself and—
FATHER: It did a lot for her.

Comments: The father semanticizes mother's involvement in therapy.

THERAPIST: Hmm?
MOTHER: It did a lot for me—
FATHER: It did a lot for her.
THERAPIST: It did a lot for her.
MOTHER: —it helped build up my self-esteem.

Comments: This semantic frame implies a change in mother.

THERAPIST: (*to father*) Were those changes good for you?

Comments: The therapist addresses the political consequences of this semantic indication of change.

MOTHER: No. They weren't good for him. Yeah. They were good for me. —'Cause he was used to stepping on a doormat, and I was no longer available to be his doormat.

Comments: The consequences of political change in this family are being spelled out. Namely, approximately four and a half years ago she sought therapy for her depression. That led to what she believed was an increase in her self-esteem. Subsequently, three to four years ago she believed that she stopped "babying" her husband.

FATHER: I don't feel that's the truth. I don't feel that's true.

MOTHER: Just like you said you weren't drinking when you first came in here and we all four of us knew you were.

FATHER: (*Sighs.*)

THERAPIST: You think you kind of changed from being a sort of "good mommy" to him to an "angry mommy?" Is that where it's gone?

Comments: The therapist both accepts and challenges mother's suggestion that she has changed. She has changed from being "good" to being "angry," but she still remains a mother to her husband. This is a major intervention in the session that addresses stability and change through the meaningful noise of a wife "mothering" her husband.

MOTHER: Yes, I think I've cut the apron strings.

THERAPIST: No, you haven't cut the apron—you've just gone from being a "good mommy" to an "angry mommy?"

Comments: The therapist again semanticizes mother's change as a shift from being a "good mommy" to an "angry mommy."

MOTHER: Well, I'm angry, yes.

BENJI: I'm angry, too.

MOTHER: And yes—and I am a mommy in a way, because I'm telling him that he shouldn't drink and now I'm at the point where I don't care if he does drink, but he can't do it around me and my two sons because I don't want them to be disturbed any further.

Comments: The mother accepts both semantic frames regarding her position in the family—she's "angry" (a change) and she's a "mommy" (no change) to her husband.

THERAPIST: Okay, so if he can't drink around you—how do you enforce that?

Comments: The politics of calibrating husband's drinking is addressed.

MOTHER: Well, I told him that either we have to get a legal separation or a divorce if this doesn't work out.

THERAPIST: Okay. And that's—that's when you called the Institute and felt you had to do something.

FATHER: I called on my own. This was before we came to that conclusion.

MOTHER: But we had—we came to this conclusion verbally, but it's been since that the whole household—that something was going to burst open. That something—something had to change. We couldn't live with each other. He knew it and I knew it but we just never said it, but we did put it verbally into words.

Comments: The mother offers a semantic request for change.

THERAPIST: Um-hum. How long ago was that?

Comments: The therapist politically addresses mother's request for change by asking when they decided something had to change.

THERAPIST: Very recently, and since then have you been drinking more or less?

Comments: The therapist is attempting to build a clearer view of the systemic organization of his drinking behavior.

FATHER: Same.
THERAPIST: Same. It hasn't—um-hum—
FATHER: No more. No less.
THERAPIST: No more. No less. How long have you been working?
MOTHER: I've been working five years.
THERAPIST: So. Pretty much since Benji was born.

MOTHER: I started working when he was about eight months old and I never did that. See, with this one, with Little Tommy I never did that. We call him Little Tommy. I never did that, with him I stayed home until he was about four or five years old. So he always had me, so maybe this is what could be wrong with Benji, because Benji—

THERAPIST: Benji says no. He's got Tommy. (*Laughing*) Who takes care of him?

Comments: By talking about the general semantic frame of "who takes care of whom," the view of father being mothered by his wife is implicitly reinforced.

MOTHER: Who takes care of you?

BENJI: Mommy and Daddy take care of me.

THERAPIST: Daddy takes care of you?

BENJI: —takes care of me.

THERAPIST: And who else?

BENJI: And Tommy takes care of me. After I was a baby and I was older and I stayed home, then I got sick.

Comments: The therapist begins exploring who takes care of the children (political frame) and finds that Tommy is a parentified child who is often put in charge of his younger brother.

THERAPIST: You got sick too? Who takes care of you now when Mommy's working?

BENJI: No.

THERAPIST: Nobody?

FATHER: What do you do when we aren't—when we are at work? Where do you go in the morning?

BENJI: Tommy.

FATHER: Where do you go?

BENJI: School.

FATHER: Okay.

MOTHER: Did you tell her you're in kindergarten?

FATHER: You're in kindergarten?

THERAPIST: Um-hum. Is that all day? He's in kindergarten all day now.

FATHER: Until three o'clock.

THERAPIST: Until three o'clock and then—

FATHER: Big brother picks him up.

THERAPIST: —and then big brother picks him up. And before that when he was little?

MOTHER: He was in a day-care center.

THERAPIST: He was in a day-care center.

Comments: Again, the therapist's discussion about "care" of Benji solidifies the general theme of care in the family, which includes mother taking care of father. Having reemphasized this theme, the therapist will return to addressing the drinking.

THERAPIST: Um-hum. Lily, you think that if the drinking were to stop, your problems would be pretty much over?

Comments: The consequences of change are again addressed.

MOTHER: Umm—at this point I don't—I don't know. I don't know, because I feel that the drinking is symptomatic of other problems that he has. I think he's a very troubled person. I think he has a lot of problems.

Comments: The mother pours out a series of explanatory semantic frames.

THERAPIST: Well, how did they become your problems and the family's problems? You know—a lot of people have a lot of problems.

Comments: The therapist requests information about how the semantic frame of "father's drinking problem" is related to the semantic frame of "family problems." Note that the information needed to answer this question successfully may provide additional clues about family politics.

MOTHER: Okay. Well, I guess because we allowed them to. He had a dominating personality in the house. He never wants to do anything with us. Right? We always like to go out. He never wants to go anywhere. He dampens the spirit in the house. Don't you think so, Tommy?

TOMMY: I don't know.

Comments: This exchange possibly indicates a coalition between the mother and her first son against the father.

MOTHER: He hollers and he screams. I holler and scream too—

THERAPIST: Gets angry? He gets angry easily?

MOTHER: Yeah. I don't snap at the kids all the time like he does. I holler and scream because . . . maybe they didn't do anything wrong . . . but he just snaps at them. Or maybe you see it differently, I don't know.

Comments: Most of the mother's responses are semantic frames about family politics. Here, the father's unpleasant behavior with the children is underscored. The therapist subsequently asks the father how his behavior changes when he drinks. Over and over the therapist is looking for ways to get at the social consequences of the drinking behavior.

THERAPIST: Are you better natured when you're drinking or when you're not drinking?

FATHER: (*Sighs.*)

THERAPIST: Do you know?

FATHER: When I'm not drinking.

THERAPIST: Are you?

FATHER: Anytime I'm drinking it's because I got a problem I cannot resolve, so I drink—

THERAPIST: No, but what I want to know is what the drink does for you, does it make you feel better or worse? I mean—are you more aggressive when you drink or when you don't drink?

FATHER: Aggressively I'm not either way. It's—the only way I get aggressive is—umm—she doesn't like for me to drink, so—

MOTHER: Why? Why don't I like for you to drink?

FATHER: Because—I get—because I get—sometimes I get verbal. Most of the time I want to be by myself.

THERAPIST: When you drink or when you don't drink?

FATHER: When I'm drinking—

THERAPIST: When you're drinking you want to be by yourself?

FATHER: —I withdraw—

Comments: The father has presented a social consequence of drinking: he "withdraws" as an attempt to "be by himself."

MOTHER: He gets violent when he drinks also.

THERAPIST: He gets violent also.

FATHER: Let me tell you why. See—let me explain something. Let me finish now.

THERAPIST: Um-hum.

FATHER: I go into myself and I don't interact with the family. My wife—she's trying to tell me I'm wrong for what I'm doing. As long as I'm left alone, I'm fine and then it's more or less a prodding—it's a prodding of what I've done—I've done something wrong, I'm drinking, I haven't taken care of this or I haven't—and it just works out that way.

Comments: The father is beginning to spell out the social sequence of events that politically organizes his drinking behavior. As can now be seen, father's report that he withdraws when he drinks is only part of a larger sequence of action that includes wife's efforts to prod him out and, as soon will be seen, his becoming angry.

THERAPIST: And then she comes after you, trying to get you to do stuff—

FATHER: I don't just walk in the door and—you know—go off, nothing like that. It just builds up.

THERAPIST: If you were left alone—

MOTHER: One time you did go walk in that door and go off, the time you choked me. You went off on me for no reason at all. Something that you made up in your mind and that's one night that I did not argue with you. Did I argue with him that night, Tommy?

TOMMY: No.

Comments: The mother again joins with son against father.

MOTHER: I minded my business, didn't I?

TOMMY: Um-hum.

MOTHER: And you prodded and you kept on till you had fabricated something.

FATHER: Hey, that particular night, I was off—

BENJI: I was eating peanut butter.

FATHER: You was eating peanut butter.

BENJI: And you started fighting in the kitchen.

THERAPIST (*to Benji*): You remember it well.

FATHER: He sure does.

THERAPIST: Okay, so the drinking makes you more aggressive and angry and quicker—you have a quicker trigger.

FATHER: I assume so.

THERAPIST: Would you say, Lily, that he has a quicker trigger when he's angr—been drinking. It doesn't make him happier or—

MOTHER: No it doesn't.

THERAPIST: It has a bad—

MOTHER: He gets—he told me that last time even on a binge that he wanted to be dead and he wished he was dead. He wished he would get cancer and die.

THERAPIST: This was while he was drinking.

MOTHER: This was about a week ago.

THERAPIST: When he's not drinking, what's he like?

Comments: Having explored the social consequences of drinking, the therapy will examine the consequences of not drinking.

MOTHER: Not happy.

THERAPIST: Would you say very unhappy?

MOTHER: Um-hum.

THERAPIST: How unhappy?

MOTHER: Morbid

THERAPIST: Morbid.

MOTHER: Um-hum

THERAPIST: Would you—downright depressed—

Comments: The semantic frames of husband's behavior when he's not drinking have been constructed: not happy, morbid, and depressed.

MOTHER: Um-hum.

THERAPIST: And then what do you do? Do you try to cheer him up or—does that upset you?

Comments: The therapist requests political information about what mother does when her husband is not drinking and is depressed.

MOTHER: Sure and he tells me to mind my business, and—you know—

THERAPIST: How do you try to cheer him up? What do you do?

MOTHER: Well, I'll talk to him or I'll say what happened during the daytime or I'll start talking about little—something that's going on with somebody else or something in my family or something the kids did, and he's just not interested at all.

THERAPIST: Um-hum. You can't—you just don't know how to cheer him up.

MOTHER: No. Not anymore I don't. I don't think I ever did.

THERAPIST: You don't think you ever did, there was no time. How about you, Tommy, would you know how to cheer him up if he's really down?

Comments: The therapist begins building the semantic view that part of the problem is mother's inability to cheer up her husband. This semantic frame will be used to explore how other family members attempt to cheer him up: mother unsuccessfully attempts to interest him by telling him about family and social events, Tommy says he doesn't go to him, and Benji makes more of an effort to cheer him up.

TOMMY: I don't bother to.

THERAPIST: You don't bother to, you're just too angry with him. Hmm?

TOMMY: Not really angry, but I sense when he's drinking. When he's drinking I don't do nothing, just walk off.

THERAPIST: And when he's not drinking and he's just sort of sad and depressed—

TOMMY: I don't really go to him. If I want to—if I want to talk to him I can talk to him, but if I don't want to talk to him I don't say anything to him so there's no need for me to go to him at all.

THERAPIST: How about Benji, does he get into it, does he try to cheer him up?

TOMMY: Yeah. Benji does. Benji is a very sensitive child.

THERAPIST: He's very sensitive to his dad.

TOMMY: To everybody.

BENJI: I want to speak my mind.

FATHER: You want to speak your mind, go ahead.

THERAPIST: Yeah. How about you?

FATHER: What about you?

THERAPIST: You try to cheer your dad up when he's feeling bad?

BENJI: No. I was at the house and Daddy was going out the house. He was never there. And the car got broke so we was there and Mommy said the car's not working, so the car was broken.

THERAPIST: The car was broken? Did that make Dad angry?

BENJI: No—Mommy angry.

Comments: Again, we could hypothesize that Benji is more joined with his father.

THERAPIST: It made Mommy angry. (*To father*) Do you ever talk to anybody about your depression?

Comments: The therapist shifts to widen political frame that addresses other people who may have helped him with his depression. We find that he had previously been in therapy and under medication.

FATHER: Once, yeah. I went to a therapist.

THERAPIST: Yeah?

FATHER: The direction or whatever—we just didn't seem to resolve anything. We talked—we talked and she made certain things aware, but it never cleared up what was making me hurt, see. It was like putting a Band-aid on something very bad and she could—we could never get into it—you know—never could.

Comments: Again, the father implicitly suggests the meaningful noise that there is a riddle underneath his drinking.

THERAPIST: Never.

FATHER: We talked about it. They tried to give me medication for depressions.

THERAPIST: They did put you on medication.

FATHER: Yeah. They gave me medica—I was on medication for about—I was on medication for about two months.

THERAPIST: Yeah, when was that?

FATHER: This was about last April, somewhere around then.

THERAPIST: Oh, so—and did that help?

FATHER: Yeah. It helped. It—it—it broke through the—I don't know if—to be honest I really can't say if it helped or not. All I know is that I came out of the depression.

THERAPIST: And you stopped taking the medication.

FATHER: And I stopped taking the medication because I lost—I just started losing faith in the system that they were putting together. It was a Dr. Smith and a therapist, and the doctor—all he would do was take my—take the blood to see how much chemicals were in my system and Miss Jones and I would sit down and we'd discuss how I felt today, whether it was a "blue day" or an "up day" and—

THERAPIST: Did you see a difference in him when he was taking the medication?

MOTHER: I just noticed that he—he slept more and I guess there was a difference in him. There was somewhat of a difference in him. I don't remember now, because everything has happened since and it's clouded—you know—I've been under so much stress that I guess I don't—I don't acknowledge it anymore. I just put it in the back of my mind, because with him it's up one day, down the other day. He does something and you just never know what to expect from him. He does good for about three days and then after that he goes right back to the same routine again. So, I guess there was an improvement when he was going there, but he looks for miracles and I told him the miracle's within yourself—

> *Comments:* The mother slips in a clue about the temporal cycle organizing the father's problem behavior: three good days followed by a problematic episode.

THERAPIST: Was that Lithium you were on? Do you know? Do you know?

FATHER: I really can't remember. Little tiny orange pills.

THERAPIST: And they took your blood test what, once a month or so?

FATHER: Took my blood test—took a blood test every two weeks. Every two weeks they'd take blood tests and see how much was in my system.

THERAPIST: Did you continue drinking while you were on it?

FATHER: No.

THERAPIST: No.

FATHER: I didn't drink. Then I was confident that I was going in the right direction and I felt that if I was going to seek help, I'd find it, but I didn't get what I wanted. I guess—I—I—I don't know—I didn't resolve what I needed. Let's put it that way.

THERAPIST: Okay. Now clearly I'm not going to be able to do anything much in this half hour—

FATHER: Sure.

THERAPIST: —Just a kind of getting to know each other. I'm going to ask you to come back next week. Can you get here earlier?

> *Comments:* The therapist semanticizes the first session as a social introduction.

MOTHER: Well,—

THERAPIST: I stop at seven.

MOTHER: Oh—yeah, yeah, yeah I can get here by six o'clock. Is that too late?

THERAPIST: Well, six o'clock the outside latest so that we can have the hour.

FATHER: Yeah, we can make the six o'clock.

MOTHER: Well, I'll be coming from—I—I took off today, but I will—I'll be coming from Forty-fifth Street so I can get down here in no time. I can get down here about ten to six.

FATHER: I can be as early as needed, because I'm off at three-thirty. I'm home at four-thirty.

THERAPIST: See if you can get here at five-thirty, so that we can have a good hour and a half—

MOTHER: See, I get off at five-thirty.

THERAPIST: Can you get off a little earlier, just this one time?

MOTHER: Okay. All right.

THERAPIST: So that we can have a good hour and a half to really look at what's going on. It's not—you know?

FATHER: Sure, it's not fair—

THERAPIST: The problem's been going on for a long time—let's see if I can be some help to you. Okay? So, come in at five-thirty next week, and then after that we'll try to adjust the time—

MOTHER: Okay.

FATHER: Okay.

THERAPIST:—and it won't be every week, necessarily, or I don't even know if I'll continue with you or somebody else, but I need a good piece of time to really see what we can do. Okay? Goodbye, Benji, it was nice to meet you.

As was mentioned in the commentary, one way of looking at this first session is in terms of the therapist gathering building blocks that may be used in the construction of a therapeutic reality. These building blocks refer to what has been called semantic and political frames of reference. The therapist has collected a wide diversity of semantic frames of reference that define problems, provide an explanation of the problems, and provide generalizations about family political patterns. The specific types of political frames included specification of problem-solving behavior, indication of coalition patterns and other social participants connected to the problem, and sequences of action that include the problem behavior(s). A partial listing of the communicational frames that were presented in the first session follows:

Semantic Frames: Problem Definition
    father's drinking
    family problems
        mother not warm and responsive enough to children
        mother withdrawn from family
        Benji's anxious behavior
        Tommy's inability to express feelings and frustration with being "let down"
        mother's and father's history of depression

Semantic Frames: Problem Explanation
    drinking causes family problems
    father's family of origin causes drinking (his father was an alcoholic)
    father drinks because something inside isn't settled

Semantic Frames (about politics)
    father is "chief problem" of family
    first son is in middle of parents' arguments
    older brother takes care of younger brother
    mother is mommy of father

Political Frames (sequential patterns)
    father drinks—withdraws and goes into himself—mother prods—father explodes (e.g., he once choked her)

Political Frames (problem-solving behavior)
    father tried AA
    Alanon
    father and mother have had therapists
    mother tells father not to drink at home; threatens divorce
    father treated for depression with medication
    mother treated for depression (presumably by talking about self-esteem)

Political Frames (coalitions)
    mother and Tommy against father
    father and Benji against mother
    mother and maternal grandmother against father

With these communicational frames or building blocks, the therapist can begin building a therapeutic foundation. The therapist, in fact, has already begun this task. She repeatedly addressed the general theme of "caring" and in particular underscored how mother is a "mommy to father." The change that mother reported in her behavior was reframed by the therapist as changing from a "good mommy" to an "angry mommy." This was a therapeutic intervention that acknowledged that although a change had occurred, their relationship basically remained the same. In addition, the therapist implied that the family's effort (particularly mother's) to cheer up father may be contributing to the problem. The therapist was careful to close the session by marking it as a beginning effort in getting to know them. In other words, although therapeutic interventions were cast, the therapist has not contextually marked them. This helps prevent the family from resisting what they might perceive as purposeful efforts to change them.

SESSION TWO

Constructing A Foundation

THERAPIST: We missed you all last week.

MOTHER: I missed coming here last week.

THERAPIST: Did you?

MOTHER: Yeah.

BENJI: *(to mother)* How you get here?

FATHER: My fault.

MOTHER: From the office, Benji.

BENJI: He take us for ice cream. We came by his car.

MOTHER: Well, I came by train.

BENJI: Well, we came by car.

THERAPIST: The three of you came together? You three came together, from home? And mother came from the office. Huh?

BENJI: I thought Mommy's going to stay home.

THERAPIST: Oh, you thought it was just you three guys coming.

BENJI: Um-hum.

Comments: This may suggest a political shift in the family—all the men appear to be joined together.

THERAPIST: Hmm. Well, what would you think of that? Would that be okay?

BENJI: Yeah.

THERAPIST: Yeah. Would you have liked that?

BENJI: Um-hum.

THERAPIST: Um-hum. That way you'd get to do more of the talking. Hmm?

BENJI: Yeah.

THERAPIST: All right, what have you been thinking about since I last saw you?

Comments: This therapy has not included an explicit contract specifying what problem is being worked on. Therefore, the therapist will not directly ask whether the father's drinking or the son's anxious behavior or the mother's self-esteem, among other problems that were mentioned, have improved. Instead the therapist will utilize the family's semantic frames in a way that attempts to reorganize their political patterns of organization. Asking what they've been thinking about enables the family to present *their* choice of communicational frame.

FATHER: You want to talk?

MOTHER: Why don't you go first?

FATHER: Well, as I said—the last time I spoke to you on the phone. I went back to AA but this time with a different outlook. The times I went before I didn't think I belonged. I didn't feel it was for me and I didn't adhere to any of the rules, or I wasn't really that interested. I pretended to be. I guess I conned myself, but this time I went back, I went back to take the philosophy in hand and follow the steps and everything they said; this time I just surrendered myself, as they say, instead of using your own will. It seems to work so far. Obviously it's only a couple of—going on my second week, but it's a—it's a different feeling that I have this time about it that I never had before.

THERAPIST: (*to mother*) What's your best understanding of why he stopped last time?

Comments: Following a report of change in father's drinking, the therapist asks the family to construct a semantic frame of explanation that may provide a source of meaningful noise.

MOTHER: You mean that—the time—this last time then—after he started drinking again? Oh. Why do I think he stopped? Umm—I don't even try to think anymore about it. I don't think it's important anymore why he stopped the last time. I think what's important is that he—

THERAPIST: That he stops now.

MOTHER: —that he stops for good and that he's serious about it.

THERAPIST: Um-hum. So what do you think about his going now?

Comments: Another request for family semantics.

MOTHER: So it's still too soon for me to feel any real results, but I think, just from what he—he seems to be convinced in what he's doing now. He's—he's never gone as much as he's going now. He seems—well, so far it's been what—two weeks straight now?

Comments: Mother is expressing the possibility of "change" as well as "no change" with respect to father's drinking.

FATHER: Um-hum.
BENJI: And—
THERAPIST: You have something to say?
BENJI: Tommy.
THERAPIST: Oh, you want Tommy to talk.
BENJI: Talk, Tommy.
THERAPIST: You want to sit over here and be the therapist with me? You want to run the meeting? I bet you could, too.
MOTHER: If you have something to say, say it. If you're mad at Mommy or Daddy—you know.
BENJI: Umm—uh—let's see—
MOTHER: You don't really have anything to say, then, do you?
FATHER: Absolutely nothing.
THERAPIST: Okay. If—if in fact this is—you know—the way it's going to be and William's going to go and get the drinking in charge, then—
FATHER: That's just beginning. Now—I've done a lot of damage—you know—so it's going to take—it's going to take quite a while to get things—not even near what they had been in our earlier stages of marriage. It's a lot of things that I did. It's a lot of things that I've had to do for the first time. Responsibility. I was never a responsible person. And you said, the last time we were together—"tired of being mommied." And I was pissed, actually.

Comments: The father indicates he is trying to change in terms of being "responsible" (a semantic frame). In addition, he implies a semantic explanation of his change that has to do with rebelling against what the therapist had said.

THERAPIST: I thought you were.

Comments: If the father is rebelling against the therapist, then this response might step up the intensity of their relationship.

FATHER: I disguised it pretty well, 'cause I'm a pretty crafty individual. I thought I was. The drinking mentality makes me—
BENJI: Mad.

FATHER: —and at that point I was drinking, so I was really off the wall. You know? But the more I thought about what you said, the more I was aware that that was the truth of the whole thing.

Comments: The father suggests that the therapist was on target and implies that her analysis has helped change him.

THERAPIST: (*to mother*) I'm just wondering how much optimism you still have.

Comments: The therapist again requests mother's reaction to father's reported changes.

MOTHER: Well, it's kind of hard to have optimism when you've lived with an alcoholic as long as I've lived with him. I've been let down many times. I've had one hundred percent faith in his ability and I've had one hundred percent faith in what he has told me, and when you are constantly let down about the same situation, or when you're constantly told a nontruth, you just don't get that happy, that soon, that fast. I mean—he's really got to prove to me this time. It's going to take more than a week or two weeks. It's going to take— he's really going to have to prove to me—like being more responsible with his boys. Doing more for me, taking more of a responsible role as a father, as a good role model father in the family—
THERAPIST: So the key word is "responsible."

Comments: "Responsibility" has been constructed as a semantic building block. Also note that mother and Tommy (in Session 1) have both expressed their concern over being "let down" by father.

FATHER: Part of it.
MOTHER: "Normal," because it has not been a normal relationship—his part in the family structure. It hasn't been. It's been abnormal.

Comments: A semantic frame about family politics.

FATHER: That's true.
THERAPIST: (*to Tommy*) Um-hum. What have you been thinking?
TOMMY: Lately, he's been doing okay.
THERAPIST: Hmm?

TOMMY: Lately my father's been doing okay. I don't have anything to say.

THERAPIST: You have nothing to say.

FATHER: Another wait and see. (*Laughs.*)

THERAPIST: Oh well, that's—that's—isn't that pretty—

FATHER: At least, it's—that's more than I expected, actually. I didn't expect that much.

MOTHER: Well, by him drinking, I have problems with little Tommy now, because he don't want to—I always have to stay on him about doing work in the house and—

TOMMY: You're really on me now.

Comments: Recall that Tommy had been seen in the first session as in-between mother's and father's arguments. As father's drinking problem changes, one social consequence is that Tommy produces problem behavior that draws his mother's attention toward him (and away from the father). The mother now argues for her son to do his work, rather than argue that father be responsible.

MOTHER: I guess he sees his father getting away with it so he feels that he can get away with it also, so he has nothing to say but it's still affecting everyone in the house, and this morning Benji says to me that he's mad with his father and he doesn't want me to drink beer, because if you drink beer you get drunk and he told me that he wanted me to tell his father that. He didn't want to tell him. So I said, "Well, why not?" He said, "Because that's your husband." I said, "Well, why can't you, that's your father." He said, "Yeah, but I can't talk to Daddy." So this was just—

THERAPIST: He told you he doesn't want you to drink beer, because it sets a bad example for William? For his dad?

MOTHER: No. He feels that drinking beer is a terrible thing now, because you get drunk like Daddy. So that makes me feel abnormal. Now, if I take a beer, I'm not an alcoholic so, I mean, that's more stress on me now. Now it's something else that I have to be saintly about.

THERAPIST: Not taking a beer. Hmm?

MOTHER: It's still abnormal for me. I mean it's not a normal situation. You know, some people do have a glass of wine occasionally at home, or a Heineken or whatever they want to, now I have to be I careful with that, because I see how my child interprets that.

FATHER: I would pass though, I'm the one who has the problem. Not you. He don't mind—he doesn't mind you drinking. He just doesn't want it in the house for fear that it being around me, that I'll start drinking again. Which is—it's understandable. It's understandable. I don't think it'll be a permanent thing. Yes. (*Benji whispers to father.*) You don't have to whisper. We're here to talk, Benji, we're here to talk.

THERAPIST: Okay, I had—since we had two weeks between—I had some time to look at the tape, and I guess the one thing that really kind of puzzled me—that's what I wanted to talk about a little bit before, but I had other questions to really try to understand—but the thing that really puzzled me is, how it happened that when you began to feel better, when you were taking some medication, it made you feel better, you stopped.

Comments: After hearing reports of the father's present improvement and eliciting some family semantic frames that explain his change in drinking, the therapist requests a historical semantic frame regarding how he accounted for his improvement in the past.

FATHER: I stopped because I was trying—I've always been searching for a cause of me feeling depressed, and I assumed that if I went to have some therapy that that might lift the cloud—

THERAPIST: It would tell you why.

FATHER: It was more—to me, I've been searching for an answer. Why am I depressed? I mean—nobody else is depressed constantly. I mean—it's very depressing to be depressed all the time. You know? You smile, but you're not happy. You're in a crowd, but you feel lonely. It's—you know—I've been fighting—so when I drank I just adapted the "I don't give a damn" attitude. I didn't do anything.

Comments: The father had presented this frame in the first session—his search for an answer.

THERAPIST: Okay, but when you were taking the medication you said you felt better. You felt less depressed.

FATHER: I felt less depressed, yeah. I felt less depressed. I don't know if it was because of the willingness or the hope that—I don't actually know if the medication did what it was supposed to do. I hoped so much; wanted it so much. I don't actually know if it really did that much. I stopped drinking and I thought that it was working and—

THERAPIST: What did you think it would do for you?

FATHER: I thought it would calm me down. At that particular time I was very hyper. I was pacing. I couldn't sleep well and I felt like I wanted to commit suicide, but I never had the courage to do anything like that so I'd always be around to—but drinking myself to death, see, that was painless. So, that was the out, and I stopped drinking because I really wanted to give it a shot. It wouldn't be fair to cheat. So I wanted to see if this thing would actually work and I came to a point where it just seemed to be going in circles.

THERAPIST: And part of what was going on with you, talking to the therapist was something that didn't seem to give you the answers you were looking for.

> *Comments:* The therapist is pinning down the semantic frame that "father has been looking for answers." We can now predict that the session will include a search for semantic frames that may provide a source of meaningful noise for the father. From what the father already said in the first session, this may involve looking at his family history.

FATHER: No. Didn't give me the answers I was looking for, because the answers I was looking for were within me. I found—now I think I found what the whole problem was. The whole problem was I was depressed with my work situation. I was depressed with my productivity. I was depressed with the fact that I never accomplished anything. I start—I'm a great starter, but I haven't finished anything in the thirty-five years that I can recollect, so that's somewhat depressing and—growth. It was brought to my attention that growth is important and I seen my wife after she went to therapy. Gradually, I've seen a change and I see her blossom and mature into a serious individual, and now I say to myself, now why can't you move? What's the problem? You know? So I got depressed, and then I went and started drinking again 'cause—I figured if I drank enough I'd chase her away and the burden that has been burdening her down all this time will be relieved.

THERAPIST: Okay. But what impresses me also, looking at the tape, is that this is a family that has very high expectations of yourself and of each other. Would you say that was true?

Comments: The therapist is generalizing (and contextualizing) the family's behavior in terms of "high expectations . . . of each other." Note that previous family descriptions supporting this generalization include themes of "responsibility," "proof of change," and "finishing what one starts." The therapist will continue constructing a therapeutic foundation for the family based on this general semantic frame. For instance, the therapist will now ask the son what he intends to do with his life. Note how this conversation further builds and intensifies the semantic frame of "high family expectations."

TOMMY: (*Nods yes.*)
THERAPIST: And you, too, you've got pretty high expectations for yourself. Hmm?
TOMMY: Yes.
THERAPIST: Yes? What are you going to do with life?
TOMMY: I'm thinking about being a lawyer, a football player.
THERAPIST: Going to school on a football scholarship, or—
TOMMY: No.
THERAPIST: No.
TOMMY: Educational scholarship.
THERAPIST: Educational scholarship. You're a pretty good student. Hmm?
TOMMY: Yes.
THERAPIST: Um-hum. Yeah. That pleases you?
FATHER: Immensely. That's the one thing that really makes me happy.
THERAPIST: Um-hum. Yeah, but—I mean—this is definitely a family in which goals and expectations are all very important. You have them for the children and you have them for each other and you have them for yourself. Hmm?

Comments: After the therapist got the family to discuss the son's goals, she used that conversation to exemplify the reality of "expectations." One could propose that the general theme of "expectations" is providing a direction for positively connoting a wide variety of the family's descriptions, including those about father's problem behavior.

FATHER: Yeah. I'd say so.

THERAPIST: Yeah. And I guess partly what happens between the two of you often is that Lily's expectations for you are always very high and then there's some sense of letdown and disappointment. Hmm?

Comments: Having solidly built the semantic frame of "family expectations," the therapist can use it as a way of talking about political patterns of interaction. Note that the theme of "high expectations" is also becoming associated with the theme of "disappointment."

FATHER: Well, I—I—I create—the more you're around me, the more you'll understand. I'm very good with words. I'm very good—I'm a "master manipulator." Let's put it that way. And I do it to cover up my inadequacies.
THERAPIST: Well, look, William, so am I, a "master manipulator."
FATHER: Yeah, well—
THERAPIST: So maybe we will be a good match for each other.

Comments: The therapist uses this opportunity to amplify her symmetrical relationship with the father so that it may be used as a resource later in the sessions.

FATHER: I do think we will. (*Laughing*) That's why I was glad to come back, because you're okay.

Comments: The way in which the therapist has framed their symmetrical relationship has been in terms of their similarities—they're both "master manipulators." This similarity has joined them, as well as built a frame that encourages father to rebel and express his autonomy.

THERAPIST: Okay. I want to see if we can—just a little bit—I don't do too much history taking. I mean—I don't really—but— (*Having stated that she doesn't "do too much history taking," the therapist goes to a corner of the room and pulls out an enormous stack of poster paper for taking notes.*)
BENJI: (*Raises hand.*)
THERAPIST: You think you're in school? Okay, what can I do for you, sir?
MOTHER: Benji, come on, don't act retarded. What's wrong?

BENJI: Nothing.

THERAPIST: When you get really bored—and it's very hard to sit still when you're seven years old—there's a box in the corner that's full of—sort of junk, toys, things. If you'd like to look in it, you can do that.

FATHER: Yeah?

THERAPIST: Just sort of quietly. Okay? Don't bang around too much because then—the videotape—okay? Can you open it? So maybe you can help him get it open and—he can do it, okay. Good. I want to know a little bit about your families, so I'm going to start with you a little bit, just so I know and see what the two families are like. You mentioned your mother last week, but said nothing about your dad.

> *Comments:* The therapist is exploring family history for possible sources of meaningful noise. The foundational theme of "high expectations" will be used to organize this information. More specifically, the therapist will use family history as a means of further solidifying the therapeutic foundation of "high expectations" and its association with "disappointments." The literal content of what they say is less relevant to the therapist than the steering of what they say to build further examples of "high expectations" and "disappointments." As will be seen, mother states that her father "wasn't what I would call high expectations." After she describes the men in her family of origin, the therapist asks, "Which of these three men had the high expectations?" We find that her first stepfather had high expectations for her to succeed academically, and we later find that her mother had high expectations for her to marry the right man as well as to finish college. We also find that she has been a disappointment to her mother and stepfather in having married someone they thought was the wrong man.

MOTHER: No. I wasn't raised by my real father. I was raised by my stepfather.

THERAPIST: Okay. What happened to your father?

MOTHER: Well, I guess he's dead now. He was one of these absentee fathers. He was never around.

THERAPIST: What—he left the family or he just was never around?

MOTHER: It was a big mystery.

THERAPIST: Mystery.

MOTHER: I've never really been told formally what happened; it was just that he was never there and I remember having a stepfather.

THERAPIST: Um-hum. You don't remember him at all.

MOTHER: No. I met him when I was about twelve years old and my stepfather didn't want him to come around, so I had only met him and his family for about three times.

THERAPIST: And the first time when you were twelve.

MOTHER: When I was about twelve. Yeah.

THERAPIST: All right, so you must remember him.

MOTHER: Oh, yeah. I half remember what he looks like.

THERAPIST: Yeah? What was he like?

MOTHER: Well, he wasn't—he wasn't what I would call high expectations, for a father. I think he was a drug addict.

THERAPIST: Oh, he was.

MOTHER: I think he was. Going by hearsay. I don't think he worked consistently.

THERAPIST: Not a very responsible man. Hmm?

MOTHER: I just think he was a poor role model, when I did meet him.

THERAPIST: And not a responsible man.

MOTHER: Not at all, because if he was responsible he would have taken care of his family and he would have seen me even though him and my mother were not together.

Comments: The mother's discussion of her father has already reinforced the family reality of "high expectations" and "disappointment." The therapist will therefore direct her to discuss other family members.

THERAPIST: You were the only child they had together?

MOTHER: Yes. Um-hum, but I have a brother.

THERAPIST: Stepbrother, or half brother—

MOTHER: Half brother.

THERAPIST: Um-hum. And then your mother remarried?

MOTHER: Yes. She had been married twice.

THERAPIST: Twice after that. And the man you remember as your father was the first one? The second one.

MOTHER: Well, I'm kind of attached to both of them.

THERAPIST: You are.

MOTHER: It was like having two fathers.

THERAPIST: Um-hum. Okay. So you grew up largely with—who's—with whom. What was his name?

MOTHER: Okay, I grew up with—she was with my first step-father until I was about eleven years old, then after that she remarried right away and I grew up with my second stepfather. Until now she's still with him.

THERAPIST: And the brother was born to—

MOTHER: The first stepfather.

THERAPIST: Aha. And how much younger is he than you?

MOTHER: Well, I'm thirty-three and Robert is twenty-eight, so it's about five-and-a-half years' difference.

THERAPIST: Uh-hum—and what's he up to these days?

MOTHER: Which one? My brother?

FATHER: He works for me.

THERAPIST: Yes?

FATHER: I got him into the sanitation business.

MOTHER: He's not doing much with his life at all.

Comments: Some therapists might get distracted by this comment and point out to the couple that mother has indirectly "disqualified" her husband by semantically framing her brother's job with her husband as meaning that her brother is "not doing much with his life." Silverstein's principal interest at the moment, however, is upon steering and organizing their discussion of family history to build up the foundational themes of "high expectations" and "disappointment." Note that in this particular case, the mother's comment about her brother actually supports the theme of "disappointment."

THERAPIST: No?

MOTHER: No. Now—there was a big mystery with what he was doing and now my husband has him doing some trade work. So—construction trade work.

FATHER: He's doing—he's starting to do something.

THERAPIST: Um-hum. Is he in trouble? Drugs, alcohol, anything?

MOTHER: No. No drugs, no alcohol, just not ambitious.

THERAPIST: Just can't seem to find a place for himself.

MOTHER: He's spoiled.

THERAPIST: Um-hum. Which of these three men, would you say, had the high expectations and—

Comments: This question frames all of the mother's discussion about men in her family in terms of "high expectations" and "disappointments."

MOTHER: My first stepfather.

THERAPIST: Your first stepfather. His father—Robert's father.

MOTHER: Um-hum.

THERAPIST: What did he do?

MOTHER: Well, he had his own business and he was—a—he was a very—academically, he was very astute. Schoolwork was very important to him.

THERAPIST: Oh, yes? Aha.

MOTHER: He was the one that—when I first started Catholic school, he was the one who helped teach me my primary techniques, whatever you want to call it. He was the one that instilled in me high academic achievements.

THERAPIST: He did. How did he do that? Did he help you—

MOTHER: He was very stern. He had—he expected—if I brought home an 85, it wasn't good enough. He expected me to bring in 90s and nothing less than that so—

Comments: The reality of "high expectations" is again reinforced.

THERAPIST: What was his name?

MOTHER: Robert.

THERAPIST: Oh, he was also Robert. So what happened to that marriage?

MOTHER: Well, I guess he was too stern and he was too dull for my mother, so she went on to—met someone else and she remarried, and he was the total opposite of my first stepfather.

BENJI: Grandpa?

MOTHER: He was also an achiever also. He was a salesman. They later went on and he opened up his own business also, which is very—

THERAPIST: He was another achiever.

Comments: The theme of expectations is indirectly underscored.

MOTHER: Yeah.

THERAPIST: And the message—and your mother? Did she work?

MOTHER: My mother is, was always, a go-getter, yeah. She never stayed home. She always worked. She always worked.

THERAPIST: She always worked. And was she also interested in your making it in the world and doing well and—

Comments: The theme of expectations is again indirectly underscored.

MOTHER: She was interested in—she was interested in—she didn't love—I don't think she loved me that much, but she was interested in—she always had this thing about me seeing boys. She used to say, well, if you wore socks a certain way you were considered a toughie or—umm—she told me she thought that I was better than other people and if you messed around with boys you were a bad person and she would disown me and—you know—she was pretty tough when it came to—

THERAPIST: Hmm. So in her way she had high standards for you, but it was through some—that you should marry the right man.

Comments: Again, the therapist organizes information so that it builds the view of high expectations.

MOTHER: Yeah. It was through—it was through wholeness. She—we—where even today we're not very warm. I don't kiss her. My husband will kiss her more than I do. Don't you think so?

FATHER: I used to. Not these days.

MOTHER: Well, he used to.

THERAPIST: So, what did she think when you started going with William?

MOTHER: She didn't want me to go with him, and she didn't want me to marry him.

THERAPIST: She didn't.

MOTHER: No.

FATHER: Nope.

THERAPIST: You knew that. How old were you when you two started—

MOTHER: Well, I met him when I was about sixteen, and I married him when I was nineteen.

THERAPIST: Oh, so you were very young. Hmm? And she really objected—

MOTHER: —because she wanted me to go on to college, but— I did go on and get my liberal arts, but she wanted me to go on and have a real career, like get a master's.

THERAPIST: Um-hum. Um-hum. You had finished college before you married?

MOTHER: No.

THERAPIST: You were only nineteen.

MOTHER: He was still going to college when we got married, and then I went back after I was married.

THERAPIST: You went back after you were married, but before Tommy was born.

MOTHER: Well, yeah.

FATHER: He was born.

MOTHER: He was born already, yeah.

THERAPIST: And you continued school. Um-hum. How about your stepfather, Robert, did he approve of William?

MOTHER: He wasn't around—

FATHER: He wasn't at that point where he had any say so.

THERAPIST: Which happened first? Did she divorce first or—

MOTHER: Yeah, she divorced when I was eleven.

THERAPIST: When you were eleven, and married the salesman when?

MOTHER: When I was twelve.

THERAPIST: Oh, right away.

MOTHER: Right away.

FATHER: Benji, put that away.

THERAPIST: That makes too much noise.

FATHER: Too much noise.

THERAPIST: Silent music. You think you've been a disappointment to her?

> *Comments:* Again, the specific content of what has been said is less important than the therapist's gatekeeping of family history to construct a foundation for a therapeutic reality that centers around the semantic frames of "high expectations" and "disappointment." Building this therapeutic foundation is a beginning step toward providing the family, particularly father, with some meaningful noise out of which they may construct answers and solutions.

MOTHER: So, yeah, by those standards I would say that I am—

I'm a disappointment, because she always tells me—my stepfather always tells me that I should leave him, because I have too much going—I have too much going for me to stay with him.

THERAPIST: I see—that he's the disappointment or that he's the cause of the disappointment.

MOTHER: That I can still do something with my life because I'm aggressive.

THERAPIST: Um-hum. Your stepsister is younger than Robert.

MOTHER: She's about the same age as me. She's thirty-three.

THERAPIST: Thirty-three. So, now, whose child is she?

MOTHER: She's my step—my second stepfather's daughter, from a previous marriage.

THERAPIST: Ah, yes. Okay.

MOTHER: From a previous marriage.

THERAPIST: So she's really a stepsister, not a half sister.

MOTHER: No. She is the stepsister. A true stepsister.

THERAPIST: And she lives with them in—

MOTHER: No. She lives in Georgia, but she has a home.

THERAPIST: What's her name?

MOTHER: Susan.

THERAPIST: How do you two ladies get on?

MOTHER: Well, not really too, too well. We don't—well, I don't see her as much. She's not my real sister, so there's a difference there.

THERAPIST: Um-hum. Well, both of these men, Robert and what's the other stepfather's—

Comments: Note that the discussion of her sister didn't lead to a lot of information that could directly reinforce the themes of high expectations and disappointments. Therefore, the therapist stopped discussion about that family member and turned to reexamining the stepfather.

MOTHER: Hank.

THERAPIST: Hmm?

MOTHER: Hank.

THERAPIST: Both of these men, you've gotten along with well and have liked and—

MOTHER: Well, there's been problems there with the second one that I can't go into now 'cause my two sons are here, and I don't want them to know about it with the second one but—

THERAPIST: Al right. I can imagine what that is then, right?

MOTHER: I don't want to mention it now—

THERAPIST: All right. That's all right.

MOTHER: —because my sons are here. But with the second one.

THERAPIST: With Hank.

MOTHER: Yes. Um-hum. But I think a lot of Big Robert. He comes around sometimes to see him.

FATHER: He comes around.

THERAPIST: Comes around. Is he kind of a granddad to the kids?

MOTHER: Well, he's kind of a loner, because he and my mother parted real bitterly. Real bitterly, so he'll come around once a year, maybe twice a year?

FATHER: That's about it. It would be more if we extended ourselves.

MOTHER: It would be more if I extended myself, but I've been so cutoff—I've been so cutoff from the world since he's been drinking. I've been like in an isolated shell.

Comments: Recall that the mother presented this same semantic frame about family politics in the previous session. It is now extended to include a reference to her own family of origin.

THERAPIST: Well, what would your mother think anyway, if you kept up a good relationship with Robert?

MOTHER: I don't think she would care now.

THERAPIST: She wouldn't care now.

MOTHER: She has a lot of respect for him, now.

THERAPIST: Oh, she does?

MOTHER: Since she's been married to the second one she realized what a gem he was.

THERAPIST: Um-hum. You were pretty upset by that separation.

Comments: This statement underscores the theme of "disappointment."

MOTHER: Oh, I sure was. I took that very hard.

THERAPIST: You took that hard.

MOTHER: I took that harder than my brother did.

THERAPIST: And both you and your brother stayed with mother. Hmm?

MOTHER: Well, no. Well, sometimes my brother used to stay with my grandmother who's deceased now—I mean *his* grandmother—who's deceased now, Robert's mother, and they always made over him and she was—he was like her second child.

THERAPIST: Um-hum. Did you have a good grandmother too?

MOTHER: Yeah, they told me—well, my grandmother is still alive. They tell me that my grandmother and grandfather were very good to me, but a lot of times my mother worked so I was with my grandmother till I was about five years old and she—my grandmother had a lot of children—seven children. My grandmother is very ignorant. I'm not saying that to be facetious—

THERAPIST: This is your father's mother?

MOTHER: No. This is my mother's mother. My grandmother is of an ignorant background. You know what I mean? I mean she's not aware. She's not taught and I don't mean book-taught. I mean, she's just taught about certain things, and I would say the majority of her children are a product of her and—

THERAPIST: But not your mother, though.

MOTHER: Hmm?

THERAPIST: But not your mother, though.

MOTHER: No, my mother's like—they think my mother is the odd lot. She thinks that they're retarded and she thinks she's better than them and she was always ashamed of the rest of them and they hold that against her right now. I don't get along with the majority of them right now, because they don't like me either.

THERAPIST: That's because somehow your expectations and your lifestyle is a little—

Comments: The therapist uses all of this discussion about grandmother and mother as another example of the theme of "expectations."

TOMMY: Better.

THERAPIST: And you don't see this branch of the family much at all. Hmm?

TOMMY: I used to.

THERAPIST: You did use to.

TOMMY: Yeah. We never got along, because I was into more different things than they were. They were talking about baby things and I wasn't interested in that. I was telling you—I'm going to join the football team, which I joined. And they couldn't join one, because their parents wouldn't let them join one. And I was showing them how—I was bragging about myself. I love to do that and so it made them feel very inferior to me and they didn't like me doing that.

THERAPIST: No. People generally don't go for that much. Hmm?

TOMMY: No. It was like—They gave the cold shoulder. I really didn't care about it, so—

MOTHER: He just started being close to my family about two years ago because I didn't—I didn't really go by to see my grandmother. I hadn't seen her for about two years and he was never subjected to them at an early age. Just—I would say about the past two years he started—I started this crusade, "Oh, I should be close to my family."

> *Comments:* In the following dialogue, the therapist uncovers information about the grandmother's history that relates to the mother in terms of expectations and child rearing. This leads to finding a possible clue for the positive consequence of father's drinking. Namely, we find that the father has "stepped in" between mother and son when she became too abusive.

THERAPIST: You had said something last week. You had said that your mother said—had given you some advice and said something about how you were neglecting the boys because of your concern for your husband? Was that it?

MOTHER: Yes. She said that—umm—that he's—that he's—that he's acting like my child, also she said, "You have three children," and she said, "The big ox is the one—you shouldn't care whatever happens to him, because he's a grown man and he's already—he doesn't really need you, but your two children that you brought into this world are the ones that really—really need you and it's about time you saw reality for what it was." So, when she made that statement to me I realized, Gee, she's telling the truth. I had been neglecting my two sons in always gearing into him and everything always rotated around him, him, him, him, and that was wrong, because these two are the ones that are coming up and they need me, he doesn't.

THERAPIST: Um-hum. Was it that way for her, that she concentrated on her children?

MOTHER: She didn't concentrate on me at all. She concentrated on my brother. The only way she concentrated on me was by being mean and telling me that I had to get good grades, slapping me—you know. She always told me I was mean and stubborn, because she would slap me in the face and I would still give her that—that—that look. I guess it was a look of defiance and—umm— I guess it's because maybe she had me out of wedlock. I'm not supposed to know about that, but, of course, when the baby grows up and starts inquiring about the past you can hide but so much, but my family—they don't talk about it. But I mean—I'm not stupid.

FATHER: That's what the whole problem was.

MOTHER: I'm not stupid.

THERAPIST: What was the whole problem?

FATHER: She resented—she resented—Lily represented a mistake in her life and every time she saw Lily that was the mistake that she had made at such an early age. That's why she was so hard on her about sex before marriage and so on and so forth. Well, I thought she was quite clear.

THERAPIST: She didn't want her to make the same error.

Comments: Again, a major consequence of all this talk is that it builds the theme of "disappointment."

FATHER: Sure.

THERAPIST: That was somehow her way of protecting you.

MOTHER: Well, I guess it was a form of protection.

FATHER: Yeah. In her way. In her own way.

THERAPIST: Well, from making the same mistakes.

FATHER: She changed somewhat after she went to therapy, see. Before she went to therapy she was a different person.

THERAPIST: Lily?

MOTHER: She was ignorant also. No, my mother. My mother went back to school and got her master's degree, too; she did it in education. And—

THERAPIST: Did she?

Comments: The therapist will allow this discussion to continue because it builds the view of expectations.

MOTHER: Yes. And after she went back to school she became a different person, but it was too late for me and her then, because I was already grown.

THERAPIST: This was after you were already married and grown.

MOTHER: She went back to school and she got her master's and she's—she's a different person now. Now she tells me—

FATHER: Totally different.

MOTHER: —what I shouldn't be doing with my kids and I said, "Well, you did it to me," and then she said, "Well, because I did it to you, doesn't mean you have to do it to them," but it's kind of hard to—you know—learn to reprogram yourself. It's just the same thing as an abused child is an abused parent. I mean the abused child becomes the abuser.

THERAPIST: That's true—becomes the abusive parent. You think that you do the same thing to your kids as she did to you?

Comments: The therapist inquires as to whether the mother's semantic frame of abuse relates to present family politics.

MOTHER: I was doing it with him, with the oldest one.

THERAPIST: Yeah? Tough on him and picking on him and—

MOTHER: I'm the oldest too, so maybe I—umm—maybe I some—psych—somewhere psychologically I did it to him what happened to me, but my husband used to be a buffer with that, even though he was drinking he used to come in—

THERAPIST: He would step in between the two of you.

MOTHER: I used to beat Little Tommy a lot. I don't beat Benji at all now, because I guess I've learned, since I went into therapy, a lot about myself.

THERAPIST: Yeah. And you just—

MOTHER: But he's a better child than Benji.

FATHER: Benji's spoiled, that's all.

THERAPIST: (*to Tommy*) Well, we don't know that yet; Benji's still little. Hmm? You're just too polite to tell on your mom and say that she was tough on you?

TOMMY: She was tough on me, but reading articles about people whose parents were very loose with their kids, I kind of understand and thank her for what she is doing for me, so I'm not really saying she's a really mean person. Maybe sometimes I want to go to the movies, she'll tell me no. I'll think she's mean, because that's how everybody thinks if you want to do something very bad, but if you really look at it in the long run she's been a very good parent to me—

THERAPIST: Cause she cares a lot and doesn't let you do wrong. Hmm?

Comments: Rather than reinforce the semantic problem definition of "abuse" and thereby build the foundation for another therapeutic reality, the therapist joins son in framing mother's beating him as related to her positive expectations and her efforts to do the right thing. This enables the therapist to later ask mother if anyone gives her credit for her efforts.

TOMMY: Yes. So I really can't say anything about my mother at all.

MOTHER: When I get mad I curse sometimes and it's something that I'm—I'm trying to cut down on.

BENJI: Daddy don't curse.

Comments: Another possible indication of Benji's coalition with the father against mother.

MOTHER: Excuse me?

BENJI: Daddy don't curse.

MOTHER: Well, I'm not talking about Dad right now. I'm talking about me. I don't know, just some way of releasing tension because I have always had to be picture-perfect and I've always—never been able to release any tension so I guess I've used that as one way to keep the lid from blowing off.

THERAPIST: But from the story you tell, Lily, it seems that as hard as you try to be picture-perfect that you never really got much credit for it.

MOTHER: No. I still don't.

THERAPIST: Not from mother. Hmm?.

MOTHER: No. As far as I'm concerned, not from anybody. That's why I decided I was going to delete anyone that I felt threatened my self-esteem about myself, and I built up a little armor and I feel that if anyone is threatening me, or if I feel that anyone has negative vibes towards me, I don't want to be bothered with them. I'm not going to be—I'm not sent down here to be a saint.

Comments: One could see the mother as constructing a semantic frame that explains her withdrawal as a way of protecting herself from disappointment.

THERAPIST: And how do you accomplish that? How do you do that?

MOTHER: I just blot those people out of my life, now. Just is a closed door.

THERAPIST: Like you cut them off.

MOTHER: Emotionally.

THERAPIST: Have you done that with your mother?

MOTHER: Somewhat, yeah. But she still has control over me. I still care what she thinks.

THERAPIST: Aha.

MOTHER: And that bothers me sometimes, because I still feel that I'm a victim. I still feel as though I'm a slave to her—

THERAPIST: To what she thinks.

MOTHER: —because I can't totally cut the umbilical cord.

Comments: Recall the political frame put forth in the first session that depicted Lily and her mother as part of a coalition against William. The therapist now has some clues to how to begin altering that coalition.

THERAPIST: What would you have to do to win her approval now, do you think?

MOTHER: Well, I guess right now maybe if I married another man—went further in my career and married a man that was—that was—that was by her—by her evaluation, well off.

THERAPIST: Um-hum. Um-hum. That's hard—that's a hard kind of thing to—

MOTHER: She even called me on the phone and told me, "Oh, I went to a reader and the reader told me that you were going to get married again." She told me the reader—reader told her I was going to get married again to a well-off man, so I mean—you know—that's—that's kind of a way of telling you—you know—I don't—you know—I don't approve of the marriage that you have now.

THERAPIST: And that means I don't approve of you, hmm? And do you argue with her about that? Or what.

Comments: The therapist makes an intervention here, reframing grandmother's disapproval of her daughter's marriage as the same as disapproval of daughter. This semantic frame helps husband and wife to politically join against the wife's mother.

MOTHER: Not now I don't.

THERAPIST: Hmm?

MOTHER: Not now I don't, because he's been so weak he's proven to my mother and my stepfather that they were right all along and that's way—

THERAPIST: Well, that's very nice of him, isn't it?

Comments: The father's drinking behavior is positively connoted as contributing to family politics.

MOTHER: Oh, oh yeah. See, I fought all along—
THERAPIST: Very cooperative of you, William.
FATHER: Certainly.
MOTHER: I fought all along trying to prove they were wrong. That's why I stayed in the marriage.
THERAPIST: You have to prove that—you have to prove them wrong.

Comments: We now find that the mother's remaining in her marriage provides a way of proving her parents wrong. The therapist tries to build a semantic frame that helps join the couple, but does not yet completely succeed.

MOTHER: Sure. I mean—
FATHER: Not only that, isn't it—is it not worthwhile to—to—to—it's just that I don't seem to get it together. I haven't up until now. Let's put it that way. If—if there wasn't something there that you saw, obviously you wouldn't have stayed around that long.
MOTHER: Well, you always had high dreams, but you never put it together.

Comments: The theme of high expectations is reintroduced as "high dreams."

FATHER: Trust my dreams.
THERAPIST: Well, she also—she has—she doesn't give up easily. Lily doesn't give up easily.
MOTHER: No, I'm persistent.
THERAPIST: You're persistent, you're a fighter.
FATHER: Yes. She is.
THERAPIST: Hmm?
FATHER: She is. Yeah.
THERAPIST: So she's not going to give up on you that easily either.
FATHER: Not until I come to the end. Like she says she has a way that once she has enough and she shuts you off, then there's no turning back on.
THERAPIST: Then it's hard—oh, no turning back. It's hard to turn back.

FATHER: It would be impossible unless—when she turns her family off, I say to her, "Gee, you should keep in touch" and softened it a little bit, but there's nobody on my side to soften it for me, so once it's gone, it's gone.

THERAPIST: Um-hum. Let's look at your side just for a minute.

Comments: The therapist turns to exploring the father's family of origin. We can expect that this historical information will also be used to construct the therapeutic foundation of "high expectations" and "disappointments."

FATHER: Um-hum.

THERAPIST: Umm—last week Lily said your father was an alcoholic?

FATHER: Yeah.

THERAPIST: Is he still living?

FATHER: No, he died of cancer at thirty-six—forty-six. I think he was forty-six when he died.

THERAPIST: At forty-six? He was forty-six years old, or—

FATHER: Yeah. Forty-six years old.

THERAPIST: Um-hum. How long ago was that?

FATHER: Gee, had to be about, say twenty years.

MOTHER: Fifteen years ago.

FATHER: Fifteen years?

THERAPIST: So you never knew that grandfather?

MOTHER: Excuse me?

BENJI: I said, me and Tommy and Daddy's a baby.

FATHER: Um-hum.

BENJI: Not Mommy. Mommy's the mother.

THERAPIST: Mommy's the only grown-up in this family?

BENJI: Yup. (*Family laughs.*)

THERAPIST: Poor Mommy, that's a tough job.

FATHER: It's a tough job is right.

Comments: The semantic frame constructed in the first session has been reintroduced by Benji.

THERAPIST: So he died about fifteen years ago and you two were already married or not?

FATHER: No, we were going together at that time.

THERAPIST: You were going together and he got sick and—

MOTHER: From alcoholism.

FATHER: Mmmm—alcoholism—Benji sit down. Please, sit down. From alcoholism, a combination—my father died of a broken heart, that's what killed him.

MOTHER: He was a weak man.

THERAPIST: Well, it takes a weak man to die of a broken heart, or a romantic one?

MOTHER: He was a weak man. I see him as being a weak man.

THERAPIST: What happened? What's the story?

FATHER: Well, he got married to my mother and for some reason or another—well, not for some reason or another—she just realized that he wasn't going anywhere and she—she left and she took me with her—

Comments: The themes of expectations and disappointment are reinforced.

THERAPIST: Were you also an only child there?

FATHER: Yup—and she took me with her and she had to go to work, so she left me with people and I had a traumatic experience when I was young. I don't remember it. My grandmother told me. They came and got me—my grandmother; my father's mother, and took me away from her, because I was very ill from my mother leaving me on people while she was trying to get work and they abused me and so on and so forth.

Comments: The similarities between the husband's and wife's families of origin might tempt some therapists to build a therapeutic reality that would focus on helping each spouse "work through" previous traumatic experiences. Silverstein, however, avoids such a direction and remains focused on gatekeeping information about family history in a way that builds the foundational themes of expectations and disappointments.

THERAPIST: Um-hum.

FATHER: So my grandmother took me—came to the rescue and she raised me. My father lived in the house, but he never worked that often. He never was any role model. Pop was just—when he died there was no emotion, actually. I tried to, because I didn't want people to think, "Gee, this guy don't have no feeling," so I tried to get into the act that there was something there, but I resented him, I hated him—

THERAPIST: Let me just get the details of this, William. You were how old when your mother left your dad?

FATHER: I was about two then.

THERAPIST: You were that little. And her story is that she left him because he was a weak man?

FATHER: I never got her story. We never spoke. The only time I saw my mother was when my father died and she asked me— At the funeral she came to me and said, "I am your mother and I hope you don't hold it against me for what happened. At least you should hear my story."

THERAPIST: She boarded you with people while she worked.

FATHER: While she worked, yes.

THERAPIST: And then your father's mother came and rescued you.

FATHER: They heard about it—somebody—somebody in the neighborhood told her how bad I was being treated so she came and got me.

THERAPIST: Well, what kind of lady was she—Grandma?

FATHER: A super lady.

THERAPIST: A super lady.

FATHER: Very dynamic.

BENJI: Superman.

THERAPIST: Super lady.

FATHER: Yeah, she was.

THERAPIST: What's—what's a super lady like?

Comments: The therapist, by repeating the expression "super lady" and by asking questions about it, builds up its importance in the therapeutic reality.

FATHER: Well, she was very giving. She'd do anything to please me. Let's put it that way. And I don't say "super" because she did what I wanted her to do; she was just a good individual.

THERAPIST: She was a good individual. Was there a grandfather too?

FATHER: No. That's another mystery. I don't know what happened there. All I know is that my father was there and—there's pictures in the thing that I still have of this so-called individual that I assume was my grandfather, but—

THERAPIST: But what happened to him or how he disappeared or—

FATHER: Obviously it was something not to be discussed, so I never dove into it.

THERAPIST: Um-hum. And you lived in the house with grandmother and your father and you and who else?

FATHER: And my great aunt. My aunt—my wife's sister—my—mother's—my grandmother's sister and my grandmother and—there was three, actually, when I first moved in. There was Aunt Bessie and she was my mother's sister, Aunt Ida, my mother's sister, and my grandmother.

THERAPIST: Three strong ladies. Hmm?

FATHER: They were three strong ladies.

THERAPIST: Three sort of super ladies.

Comments: Again, the therapist is building the importance of "super ladies," perhaps because such people have high expectations for themselves (and others).

FATHER: All of them were super.

THERAPIST: Aha—and two little boys. You and your father.

Comments: The consequence of describing him and his dad as "little boys" is that it reinforces the semantic frame that defines the present family as a "mother and three boys."

MOTHER: And Uncle Matt.

THERAPIST: Oh, there was another one?

FATHER: Uncle Matt—no, he was—he was—

MOTHER: He was an alcoholic, too. Another drunkard.

FATHER: Yeah, but he had his own thing, he wasn't part of my family. He just lived on us because—

MOTHER: His family came to live with your family because he couldn't support his family because of his drinking.

FATHER: Yeah. But that was down the road. That was later on. They—they were just nice people, you know? They were good. They were different individuals—personality-wise, totally different, but each in all equal in goodness in their own—you know—in their own self.

THERAPIST: The ladies.

FATHER: Um-hum.

THERAPIST: And the men were just—never really grew up. Hmm?

Comments: Exploration of father's family reveals that he grew up with three "super ladies" and alcoholic men who never grew up. We will see, however, that there was one exception: Uncle Jack. These frames of reference continue to build the foundation of "high expectations" and "disappointments."

FATHER: All the uncles, everybody—every male affiliated with the Thomas clan was just—either they were stuck in the bottle, or—there was only one—Uncle Jack. He was the only person who didn't drink and he made something of himself. He was a bank official and—

THERAPIST: Um-hum. Whose son was he?

FATHER: He was my grandmother's father—his brother. They were brothers. So he was—I don't know what that makes him but—

MOTHER: First cousins. They were first cousins.

FATHER: —to my grandmother. Okay? Well, he was somebody I looked up to. The only person—but he didn't come around that much.

THERAPIST: And where did you two meet?

MOTHER: In school.

FATHER: In school.

MOTHER: In high school.

THERAPIST: In high school. Um-hum. And at that point you had some pretty high expectations for yourself, too. Hmm? Or were those Lily's expectations for you?

Comments: The therapist's subsequent inquiry into their court-ship will also follow the semantic theme of "expectations." The therapist will ask the mother if she tried to "shape him up" in high school.

FATHER: Oh, in school? When I was coming out of school?

THERAPIST: Um-hum.

FATHER: Oh yeah, very, very high.

THERAPIST: Were you a good student?

FATHER: Adequate. No, I was never good. I was never a super student. I was never a—

THERAPIST: You were a serious student or not?

FATHER: No.

MOTHER: I was a serious student.

THERAPIST: Was he?

FATHER: Was I a serious student?

MOTHER: No.

FATHER: No, I was never a serious student.

THERAPIST: (*to mother*) You were.

MOTHER: Yes I was.

FATHER: She was.

THERAPIST: And at that time even in high school were you shaping him up?

MOTHER: Yeah, and then my grades starting slipping a little bit because I was—I had my interests on him, you know? I would try to help him.

THERAPIST: You would try to help him and to inspire him to—

Comments: The theme of high expectations is implied.

MOTHER: Well, he always said—he always had high ambitions, but like I say he never—he—he had—he had dreams, but he needed a catalyst to actually make it happen in reality, but he didn't deal in reality. He just dealt in dreams.

Comments: "High ambitions" and "dreams" underscore high expectations.

THERAPIST: Well, so in those—in those days, if you can remember back, Lily, would you—did you think that you could really inspire him to—

MOTHER: I thought I could change him.

THERAPIST: You thought you could change him.

MOTHER: I thought that—I thought that he had good dreams. He always wanted to be—he had—he talked ambitiously. He was—he was—he always seemed to be intelligent. Always had a very good way of talking and made you think that he knew where he was and—umm—I felt that with me—with—with my no-nonsense attitude and with his dreams that we could be a good team.

THERAPIST: Um-hum. And you did in fact start college, hmm?

FATHER: Um-hum. Which I never finished.

Comments: The theme of "disappointment" is implied.

THERAPIST: How far did you go?

FATHER: Two years. I went one year—the last year I dropped out, 'cause I knew everything at that point so I didn't—no sense in me wasting time. So, I wanted to continue in the computer industry and I got a job. Didn't make that much money. It was adequate for those days. As far as computer pay was. It was—I was right in there. If I had stayed with it, I could have done something with myself. Had one job—was okay. The second job was very good. This individual gave me opportunities to advance myself, but I had no ambition to—after the first couple of months—I just lost interest in it. See, then I started drinking martinis, 'cause I always wanted to be somebody, let's put it that way, and I was never satisfied with what I had become.

THERAPIST: Did your grandmother have high hopes for you?

Comments: The therapist recycles the theme of expectation, using the term "high hopes," back into father's history before the marriage.

FATHER: My grandmother was more or less worried about me. The outcome—she didn't know what would happen. The only thing that—she had high expectations for me, yes, because I—I could have achieved it if I had just stuck to something.

THERAPIST: Um-hum. Which one of you, do you think, has higher expectations for Tommy—for the boys, for your sons. Do you know?

Comments: The theme of expectations is now pushed forward in time with respect to addressing the parents' expectations for their boys. The therapist's questions, in effect, take the theme of expectation and address different periods in the family's history. In this way, implicit associations in intergenerational patterns are suggested (meaningful noise). For instance, following an investigation of grandmother's hopes for father, the parents' expectations for their sons are explored. As we will see, when the family provides an example of how they chose the right school for their son, the therapist switches time frames and asks mother who would have decided that in her family of origin.

MOTHER: I'm speaking for me. I want my son to be an attorney. I don't care about the football.

FATHER: Yeah, but who got him interested in being an attorney?

MOTHER: I always had high hopes for my son—

FATHER: I didn't say you didn't.

MOTHER: I always wanted him to be either an attorney or a doctor.

FATHER: I said we both had high hopes. The only thing was you were more consistent than I was.

MOTHER: When you have high hopes for somebody you—you—you make it a reality. You just don't talk about it and then go drinking into oblivion.

FATHER: Hey—well, I've got a problem. It's quite evident, I'm not saying I didn't. I'm not saying I don't—

THERAPIST: Well, it's—it's impossible that she's more ambitious for the kids than you are, right?

> *Comments:* Although this question may reveal a relevant political pattern in the family, its effect is to precipitate more discussion of the theme of "expectations."

FATHER: It's possible. Just 'cause it's my interpretation, doesn't make it right.

MOTHER: Excuse me, Benji, you just pushed past her.

FATHER: It's very possible, sure. I'm just saying how I feel. Even though she may feel greater than I do. I'm just saying I am concerned.

MOTHER: He always talked a good game, but he never went out and broke his neck and tried to get him in good schools and all that. You know. Umm—umm—like—where I always wanted to make sure that— One time he had told me he couldn't afford to send my child to a private school and he was going to take him out. I guess you don't remember that, huh?

FATHER: Of course I remember.

MOTHER: Yeah. Uh-huh. And like this other time for—I'm trying to get him into a good private high school— What is it? Mount Saint—

TOMMY: Mount Saint Helena's.

MOTHER: Mount Saint Helena's, because they have high academic standards. I was the one that put it into action. Oh sure, he talks a lot, but he's not the one that does anything. I'm the one that has to call the—umm—the—the archdiocese to find out when the tests are being taken or the other school program and find out when this test is being taken for that or—or when the scholarship tests are being taken. I always have to do everything. Otherwise it doesn't get done.

THERAPIST: In your—in the family you grew up in—in the family you grew up in would it have been your mother or Robert who would have seen to it that you had gone to the right school and did what you were supposed to do?

MOTHER: It would have been Robert.

THERAPIST: It would have been Robert, so then you expect, that is, he would be—

MOTHER: But my mother—but they—when it came to things like that they were both—Robert was more, but she was a doer also, but Robert was just—Robert was more—Robert was more, not powerful, but more dominating at that time over her, because he was more educated at that time, 'cause don't forget, she went back to school after she married the second husband.

THERAPIST: Um-hum. You know there's a sort of myth or story. I don't know how right it is, so you tell me whether you think there is anything in it. I've heard it said and there's been a lot written about the fact that black families—that generally the women are the strong ones, who run the family. Would you say that that's true?

Comments: The therapist presents the frame of "cultural myth" as a new class of meaningful noise that, incidentally, connects with the father's description of the "super ladies" in his family of origin. The therapist cycles the theme of expectation through this larger semantic frame, planting the seed that it's more difficult for a black male to be competitive (i.e., to achieve his expectations) than for a black female. In this conversation, the therapist will again introduce intergenerational patterns. For instance, when the mother's expectations for the father are introduced, the therapist turns to asking the father if the three strong ladies he grew up with nagged the men to meet their expectations. By association in the conversation, the therapist implies a connection between cultural expectations for black men and the expectations he has experienced in his family of origin and his present marriage.

MOTHER: Well, me and him were talking about this the other day. I hate to say it to a—to a—to a person not of color. You know—

THERAPIST: Yeah, right.

MOTHER: —but—umm—things are changing now, but yes,

they have been that way on the majority. Not—not one hundred percent, you do have—

THERAPIST: Absolutely, I know that.

MOTHER: —you do have a change but when you get into the psychological background of why the women are the strongest, maybe it came from slavery days when the families were torn apart and—

Comments: The mother is elaborating this semantic frame, thereby underscoring its potential importance.

THERAPIST: Oh, no. I understand really why. That there are big economic factors. That it's been easier for women to get work than for men to get reasonable work and it's been in many ways that black women are not as feared by the culture as competition. They let them have more room in the cul—I know—I know all that, but I guess my question is that—

Comments: More meaningful noise.

MOTHER: There's a lot of truism in it—I would say in a lower—in a lower—in a lower culture to a—I wouldn't say it was so much in the middle class. The black middle class, but I would say it was the lower-middle class to ghetto culture, subculture.

THERAPIST: Well, then, it's safer for the woman to take charge than for the man.

MOTHER: There is no—there's a man, but he's not a responsible man, if that's what you want to call a man. There is a male. I wouldn't say he's a man, but there is a male around the house. You still have a lot of black males that are in the subculture, that ghetto.

THERAPIST: Um-hum.

MOTHER: Ignorance. And ignorance is a state of mind that you don't have to be. It's something that you can uplift. It's something that you can do something about.

THERAPIST: Okay. Now tell me something else that is—what would it take for a black woman, like you, who has such high expectations and really wants something good to come out of life, what would it take for you to trust a man to be responsible for the family?

Comments: Having constructed the therapeutic foundation of high expectations, super ladies, and the cultural myth of black women and men, the therapist is beginning to lay the ground-work for a therapeutic intervention.

MOTHER: Well, Mrs. Silverstein, I don't think I can—right now I don't think—I think it'll be a long time before I can trust any man. I feel that the trust lays within myself. I'm a firm believer now in "God bless the child that has its own." I would say it would take a man—I wouldn't have that trust in a man—I'm just saying I perceive a man that's responsible, that takes care of his bills, that makes sure his family has what they're supposed to have in terms of food and proper shelter. I don't think a responsible man would have his family living in a subculture in a ghetto, because it's not safe, it's not conducive academically to the mind. There's no dreams in a ghetto if you've ever—I don't think you've ever been in a ghetto.

THERAPIST: Oh yes, I have.

MOTHER: I don't think you've been into a black or Hispanic ghetto. There is a difference.

THERAPIST: No. I have not been black. I mean—there is no—you know. And I—I never will really understand it, you're right. I'm not—

Comments: The therapist quickly avoids getting into an argument with the mother.

MOTHER: And there is a lot of people there—you know—people—you look at Reagan and you'd say, oh, well, times are changing— There's a lot of people—a large majority of people that are still in that culture and I feel that, sure I'm living in a—we have a nice apartment with a terrace and it's somewhat of a co-op, but I feel that I'm getting older now and it's at the foot of my doorway. You know—I feel it's time for me to be upgraded, because you can't stand still. If you stand still you're not actually standing still, you're going backwards. There is no such thing as standing still. If you're not making any progress then you're regressing, and he doesn't see it that way. He sees that time as being—like—in—what word were you using?

FATHER: I wasn't using anything.

MOTHER: It was—it was stagnant but it wasn't stagnant, it was regressing and I allowed him to let me regress also.

THERAPIST: Does she expect too much from you?

FATHER: No.

MOTHER: I don't think I expected enough from him.

FATHER: No.

THERAPIST: Well, both. Both of those things are probably true. That on one hand you expect too much and on one hand you don't expect enough.

Comments: The therapist is trying to weave the semantic theme of "expectations" into communication about their relationship.

MOTHER: Well, if I expected so much—he couldn't have done the things that he's done because I would have walked out a long time ago. I feel that I'm weak for sticking around.

Comments: This may be seen as a shift in mother's emphasis— she moves away from blaming her husband and focuses more on her own contributions to the situation.

FATHER: Hmm.

THERAPIST: Well, or just hopeful and devoted—

MOTHER: Or crazy in love, you know—

THERAPIST: Well, that's not all bad either. Hmm?

MOTHER: Well, I feel bad—

FATHER: As long as it has a happy ending. (*Laughs.*)

Comments: The father implies the possibility of a change in their relationship.

MOTHER: I feel bad about it right now. I feel good that he's in AA—you know—I don't even—I don't even want to go as far as to say that I feel hopeful, because you see I've been through this too many times. I feel as though he's let me down—too up and down—

THERAPIST: No. Don't be hopeful. No, no. That's the worse thing you can do at this point.

Comments: Olga Silverstein often suggests that clients not be hopeful. Hope may lead to behavioral efforts to make things better, which paradoxically may serve to maintain the problematic situation—an old adage of systemic therapies.

MOTHER: —I've been too up and down on a seesaw to say, "Oh, William, I'm so glad." You know—I'm sorry I can't do that. I have my feelings—I have to protect my feelings now. I'm happy for him. I don't want to be pessimistic.

THERAPIST (*to father*): Did those three strong ladies nag those guys, your father and uncle?

Comments: The therapist will draw upon family history as another way of introducing the theme of expectations.

FATHER: Constantly.
THERAPIST: Constantly. Constantly at them.
FATHER: Constantly.
THERAPIST: To do what?
FATHER: Something, anything.
THERAPIST: Anything. Go to work, get a job, be responsible, stop drinking—
FATHER: They worked—they worked. My father—he did—he had had a thousand positions which didn't pay too much and when you're in a situation like that—
MOTHER: "Jack of all trades and master of none."
FATHER: He wasn't an achiever—he wasn't an achiever, he just went to work to get any job he could get, just so they would stop nagging and he'd have his drinking money. He'd pay his little bit of money to them so they could maintain the house and the rest of the time he'd just drink.
THERAPIST: He'd just blot it out—

Comments: His father's drinking is now discussed as if it were a way of blotting out the expectations of others.

FATHER: Sure.
THERAPIST: —but they'd keep after him.
FATHER: Constantly. I mean he'd come home drunk—you know—neighbors—the neighbors—you know—and they'd just get very uptight about it so they sent him away to "Detox" many a time. He even went in on his own. There was no hope for him. I could sense in him, he was—he was—he was—I'd say totally dead. He could walk and talk, but he was dead.
THERAPIST: Do you remember feeling really sad for him?
FATHER: When he died? Oh—
THERAPIST: No, during his life, for the life he led.
FATHER: Sure, sure.
THERAPIST: Because children are usually very—like even Benji is so—feels for you and is so sympathetic and— Right?

Comments: The therapist has used family history to approach present family politics.

FATHER: He reminds me of myself at one stage in my life, but then I turned cold like he did.
THERAPIST: Well, that's kind of protection, right?
FATHER: Sure. Sure.
THERAPIST: You don't want to care, because it just hurts too much.
FATHER: Of course not. I mean—that's understandable. Very understandable. I don't have any problems with that, because I've been through that. And the damnedest thing is how could I come from a situation and—and then give off that same situation that I detested?
THERAPIST: Well, it's complicated how we manage to do—to redo the things we don't— Right?

Comments: The therapist has constructed enough semantic frames to spell out the explanation that father is replaying his own father's family dance.

FATHER: It really is.
THERAPIST: One of them is an issue of loyalty. You know? And I guess that—that somehow you were to, oh, do what all these women want you to do—you know—become a really responsible person and take hold of your life, but in some way maybe it seems a little bit disloyal to the memory of your father?

Comments: The therapist constructs a semantic frame that provides a way of talking about the dilemma the women's expectations place on him: on the one hand, there is a desire to be responsible and meet their expectations, while on the other hand, there is a desire to be loyal to the memory of his father and not to meet their expectations. Note that these two sides can be seen as addressing change and stability, respectively. The women's requests for change (in terms of meeting high expectations) are countered by loyalty and stability of cultural and family tradition.

FATHER: I know when somebody tells me to do something, I resent it.
THERAPIST: You get very—

FATHER: Very rigid. I'll do the exact opposite. I don't mean to, but I—it's like a click, actual—
THERAPIST: Well, that's also a kind of strength—you know.
FATHER: Maybe.
THERAPIST: A kind of refusal to do—and I think in many ways that black men have and—have—

Comments: The cultural myth about black men is used as a therapeutic resource to underscore the side of the dilemma that addresses that he not meet his wife's expectations. Namely, not meeting her expectations is implied as a way of being loyal to the memory of his father as well as to black men in general—the therapist will later refer to this as keeping "pride."

MOTHER: Destructive strength, though—
THERAPIST: It is destructive—
MOTHER: Self-destructive.
THERAPIST: It is destructive strength. It's not passive.
FATHER: Yeah, but you said something about how black—
THERAPIST: Right?
MOTHER: That's true.
THERAPIST: That black men fight it, because they won't do what the culture demands that they do.
MOTHER: That's true. You're right about that. You're right about that.
THERAPIST: And in a way that's pride and it's a kind of strength and it's not— It doesn't serve him well, right? There must be other ways not to do what—not to become an "Uncle Tom."

Comments: The therapist redescribes this side of the dilemma in terms of his trying not to be an "Uncle Tom."

FATHER: There's a lot of ways.
MOTHER: It sounds cute hearing you say that (*laughing*) because other blacks do call other blacks Uncle Toms.

Comments: The therapist has now constructed enough semantic frames (i.e., a therapeutic foundation) to present an intervention that spells out the political consequences of their dilemma: when the mother expects him to do something, he rebels against it as a way of feeling loyal and strong. However, since his response is a reaction to her provocation (rather than

an autonomous/spontaneous behavior), he is actually not being strong and independent. Thus, the more opportunities she provides for him to feel strong by rebelling against her, the weaker he becomes. Note how the therapeutic foundation constructed in this session embraces the cybernetic structure of stability, change, and meaningful noise:
("disappointments"/"expectations")/family history and cultural myth.

As we previously indicated, the foundational theme of "expectations" is connected to the women's requests for *change*, while the foundational theme of "disappointments" is connected to *stability* of the men's loyalty. In addition, references to family history and cultural myth have provided a source of meaningful noise. As will be seen, both husband and wife accept the therapist's interpretation. The therapist has thus moved toward a higher-order therapeutic reality where interaction rather than descriptions of simple action is the focus. What's most important in terms of therapeutic strategy is that the therapist has timed the introduction of this information in such a way as to facilitate the family's acceptance and utilization of it.

THERAPIST: Yeah, well, those are the choices. Right?
FATHER: Those that make it, they call it Uncle Toms.
THERAPIST: Yeah, well, those are the choices. Right?
FATHER: Sure, you sold out—
THERAPIST: Right. So you're really caught in a terrible dilemma. Right? You're going to be loyal to your people and not be an Uncle Tom on the one hand and yet be what the women want from you? It's really quite a spot to be in. Hmm?

Comments: Stability (loyalty to your people) and change (what the women want) are spelled out.

FATHER: Well, it was a terrible spot—I don't feel that way anymore. I do know that the women in my life played a role that I have yet to decipher, but I know something—
THERAPIST: Very powerful—
FATHER: Sure, sure they were very, very powerful.
THERAPIST: —but it's the one you fight against. It's the one that makes you feel strong when you can hold out against them.
FATHER: Maybe that's just about it.

THERAPIST: So that's one way you feel some sense of your manhood. You don't knuckle under to these women.

Comments: The therapist is redefining this aspect of their paradoxical situation. When the father accepts this definition she will approach the wife's expectations.

FATHER: Yeah. I'm a fighter. I got a lot of spunk left.

THERAPIST (*to mother*): See, the trick is, then, that the less you expect from him, the more you're apt to get.

Comments: The paradoxical effects of the mother's expectations are addressed.

MOTHER: It's not going to work with me. See, 'cause that means that I have to change my whole being and I feel now that I—I feel now that I—I shouldn't have to change because, I mean, I do change for the better. I'm not saying that, because I think growth is living. That's part of life, but I don't feel that you should change all the good things that you feel about yourself. In other words you're saying that—

THERAPIST: No. No, that's not what I said. I don't believe that either—

MOTHER: But in order for me to—

THERAPIST: Just—just as a woman I wouldn't want you to do that—you know. I said the less actual expectations you have of him, the more apt he is to take charge of his life, because he doesn't have to fight you to show—to feel his own strength.

Comments: After joining her as a woman, the therapist draws a distinction between describing what she wants her to do and describing the consequences of what she does.

MOTHER: But I'm not fighting him now, so maybe that's why he has taken charge.

THERAPIST: So, maybe. Maybe.

Comments: The mother has taken a step toward accepting this paradoxical view.

FATHER: Yeah. Now that we—I got to get something out now, since we're here talking. She's somewhat of a perfectionist—you know?

THERAPIST: She's a lot of perfectionist?

FATHER: She'll—we have a kitchen table and we have—on the chairs we have four prongs on the bottom and she's so precise that it has to be on an angle on a—I don't know what degree it would be, but if it's not on that degree she is upset. And her perfectionism— See, the difference—how far apart—I'm—I'm realizing what was making me so angry. I resent her ability to organize, because I have—I don't have that ability to organize. She runs things smoothly and I kind of resent that, in a way. You know? I mean—I did a lot of thinking about it.

THERAPIST: Yeah. But when you resent it, what do you do?

Comments: The therapist is ignoring the content of the father's criticism of mother and refocuses therapy upon father's reactions to mother.

FATHER: I rebel. Like—I have chores to do. I do the kitchen floor. When do I do it? I'm supposed to do it every weekend, but she has to remind me, you know—do that—you didn't do this or you didn't do that or you didn't do this or you didn't do that and I'm just sitting here looking—you know—I'm saying, so what?

THERAPIST: And your response is to go—

FATHER: My response is to do it when I want to do it, which is never or when I get to it.

MOTHER: Or even to go drink like he used to. He told me he was drinking because of me.

FATHER: Well, that—well, I said that, but that wasn't the truth.

THERAPIST: He knows better than that, Lily. He may say that, but he knows better.

MOTHER: Oh, I know better than that too.

FATHER: It wasn't the truth anyway.

THERAPIST: Even he knows better than that.

FATHER: It was an excuse to drink.

THERAPIST: Okay, but the rebellion is another thing.

Comments: The therapist again organizes communication and steers the focus back to the father's reactions ("rebellion") to the mother's expectations.

FATHER: That rebellion. I'm constantly rebelling about what she wants me to—she is so per—I mean she is—you don't know. She is very—she is perfect, perfect. She'll know if something is out of line. When she comes from work and somebody sat on the couch, she'll know if somebody was sitting on the couch. That's how meticulous her mind is. You know? And to me—so what do I care if somebody sat—that's what it's there for, but see, she has a set—a set way of doing things, but she's a very good woman.

MOTHER: There's a reason for that, because the last time we had a couch and carpeting there was no—there was no consistency in the house. There was no rule. There were no regulations. These kids had this house looking like a pigsty. This last time we went out and bought expensive furniture and I got rules and I'm making them adhere to them, so it has—

THERAPIST: But you see, the paradox, the funny thing is that when you rebel that way, you feel like your own man—

Comments: Everything the family presents is recycled through the therapist's paradoxical frame of reference.

FATHER: Sure do, regardless of what she thinks of me, I feel—my own man.

THERAPIST: But the paradox is that that's when you're not your own man, actually, because what you're doing is rebelling against her. Right?

FATHER: Sure. And everybody suffers because I'm not doing what I'm supposed to be doing. It's true. Right.

THERAPIST: So you're not really doing what you want to do. What you're doing is rebelling against the woman in your life.

FATHER: Um-hum.

THERAPIST: Okay.

FATHER: Very true.

MOTHER: So there's still control there.

THERAPIST: So it's still—of course, so he's still being controlled by you. That's the paradox, you see.

MOTHER: That's a good point.

Comments: Note how the therapist has defined the positive and negative consequences of the father's rebellion. On the positive side, it enables him to do what he wants by not doing what she wants him to do. This subsequently leads him to feel his strength and a sense of being his own man. On the negative side, father's rebellion is carried out by actually not doing what he really wants to do (i.e., to meet his expectations). This leaves him feeling disappointed, weak, and under the control of others. This double view of his rebellion provides another way in which stability and change can be addressed: on the one hand he must stabilize his feelings of strength and autonomy; on the other hand he must change how he rebels.

THERAPIST: All right, listen, we'll stop for tonight and—I'll see you next week and then after that maybe once every two weeks. We're not necessarily going to meet every week. As things go along we may take longer between meetings and—
FATHER: Sure.
MOTHER: Do you think therapy will help my oldest son and my youngest, because he's anxious?
THERAPIST: I think the whole thing is the whole family business, you know?

Comments: The therapist organizes the mother's communication by offering a more general semantic frame—this response attempts to sidestep any disagreement.

MOTHER: You think he's anxious because of the problem? Sure.
THERAPIST: He doesn't seem overanxious to me.

Comments: This time the therapist organizes mother's communication by disagreeing with it.

MOTHER: Well, they've turned him anxious in kindergarten.
THERAPIST: He may act out a little bit in kindergarten. He may get a little bit wild in there with the other kids, but he is not what you— He may be a little anxious and a little—yeah. Do I think that—I think that certainly—I don't know if we can help with everything—

Comments: The therapist finally organizes the mother's efforts to move the problem to Benji by taking multiple positions: "no, he's not overanxious; maybe he's a little anxious; whatever the case we might not be able to help with everything."

MOTHER: 'Cause he seems like he's dead. He seems like there's just no life in him. I'm trying to motivate him, you know.

Comments: Mother now tries to move the problem to the older son, Tommy.

FATHER: I take the blame for that, 'cause I didn't give him a good role model.

TOMMY: The thing is, I don't like people telling me what to do.

THERAPIST: Just like your father.

TOMMY: I want to do things my way and the way I like to do it. If you don't like it, I get mad if you don't like it and then I do it even more. I feel—

THERAPIST: Well, that's something that you and your father share.

TOMMY: I don't understand, because it's like, I don't want to be like my father, but in the long term I can't do things consistently like my mother can. I say I want to be—to play baseball. I make the team; next year I change my mind, I don't like it anymore. I get bored with it and I go to football. So far I'm sticking with it because I taught myself how to do it. I worked for myself. I feel that I'm so good now, why should I let it go to waste? Why work for something when you already have the ability to play, so I'm trying to keep that and ability to—I think I'd be a pretty good lawyer and writer.

MOTHER: I think you'd be a terrific lawyer. I think you have the personality for it.

TOMMY: Screen—I want to be a screenwriter too. You know, write movies, I am trying it now, seeing what I can do.

THERAPIST: Okay. But I guess there again the answer is, you find ways to be your own man without it having to be against what somebody else wants you to do. I think it's the same for Tommy.

Comments: The older son's communications, which are iso- morphic to father's, are cycled through the dilemma the thera- pist has defined.

FATHER: That's about it.

THERAPIST: That it's the same problem and I think it's a problem for most black men, okay?

FATHER: I'd say so.

THERAPIST: So in there you're—you have a harder battle than another family, for instance, a middle-class white family. They also have problems, but they're different problems.

Comments: The cultural myth is again presented.

FATHER: Right, very true.

THERAPIST: Okay, so we have to see things in context, and the world doesn't make it easier for you.

FATHER: You're telling me.

MOTHER: But you can't have—

THERAPIST: It's a much steeper hill.

MOTHER: One thing I've learned, you can't have hate, because when you hate—like Alex Haley said, he had to stop writing *Roots* when he—when he consumed all his knowledge and he started to hate, he had a total blank. He couldn't think, he couldn't function properly. You have to put the hate aside. That's what I was telling him. Instead of saying "can't," turn "can't"—drop the apostrophe T and say "can," because if you say "can't" you already closed your mind.

THERAPIST: Yeah, but you see, what they do—what they do, really is to—it's the black women who get the brunt of their anger and their rebellion.

Comments: The rebellion of the husband against his wife is now more carefully spelled out as the consequence of cultural rebellion—a frame that has the effect of positively connoting the husband's intentions (while at the same time making it possible for him to want to initiate change).

FATHER: All the time.

MOTHER: I'm trying to change it with him, 'cause I feel he's still young.

THERAPIST: Okay, folks. I'll see you next week at five-thirty?

FATHER: Yes, ma'am.

THERAPIST: Can you make five-thirty? Or six?

MOTHER: Yeah.

THERAPIST: Okay, six, I understand you can't get away from work, but you'll come at six, hmm?

MOTHER: Unless I can come in at nine that day, but it's inconsistent and I don't like to do that.

THERAPIST: All right, six is all right if you come on time at six.

FATHER: I got a good feeling about you. I think things are going to be okay.

THERAPIST: Well, we'll try. No magic here either, you know?

MOTHER: No. The magic is within yourself.

THERAPIST: Not even there.

MOTHER: No, it doesn't happen overnight. It takes time, and he doesn't have patience.

FATHER: Well, I'm adopting that philosophy in life.

MOTHER: But then I can't let that stop me because he doesn't have patience. I have my own life to live too.

THERAPIST: Yup. Okay. See you next week, then.

FATHER: Okay. It's been a pleasure.

This second session built upon the semantic and political frames of the first session to construct a particular foundation for a therapeutic reality as well as to introduce a higher-order intervention. In the first part of this session the search for understanding father's drinking led to an exploration of family history. The therapist, however, used family history politically as a way of building the therapeutic foundation that the family's life revolves around the themes of high expectations and disappointments.

Once this therapeutic foundation was firmly established, the therapist moved toward constructing an intervention that specified the paradoxical nature of their situation. Drawing upon cultural myth, family history, and present descriptions of their behavior (meaningful noise), the paradoxical effects of mother's expectations (requests for *change*) and father's rebellion (*stability* of family loyalty) were presented. The father's and mother's responses to this paradoxical announcement were utilized to provide further amplification and evidence of the paradox. The session was dismissed after both parents accepted the paradoxical definition of their interaction.

SESSION THREE

Weaving Patterns That Connect

THERAPIST: Okay. What's been doing in the Thomas family?

TOMMY: Nothing much. Oh, I passed the test in Mount Saint Helena's Academy and High School.

THERAPIST: Well, good for you. So what does that mean now, next year—

TOMMY: Next year I'll be going to Mount Saint Helena's Academy.

THERAPIST: Aha—and then from there to—

TOMMY: I don't know. Probably Harvard or Princeton.

THERAPIST: That's right through high school, now.

TOMMY: Yeah, right through high school. From there I'll go to probably Harvard or Princeton.

Comments: The general theme of expectations is implied.

THERAPIST: Well, all we have to do now is afford that, huh?

FATHER: Um-hum.

MOTHER: Scholarship.

FATHER: It's got to be some kind of a scholarship. (*Laughing.*)

THERAPIST: Well, that's pretty good. That's real nice. Um-hum. So—

MOTHER: Benji has been very anxious.

THERAPIST: He's been very active.

Comments: The therapist normalizes Benji's behavior—moving it out of a problem frame.

BENJI: I was a good boy last week.

FATHER: Last week. This is a different week.

THERAPIST: You got bored last week, but I guess your mom means at home. You've been pretty active at home, running around and—hum? Something been bothering you?

BENJI: Nope. Um-um.

THERAPIST: More than usual, Lily?

MOTHER: Well, yeah, because me and my husband had a couple of little blowups last week, especially right after we left here.

THERAPIST: Did you?

MOTHER: Yes. He was angry with me. He had an attitude with me because he felt that I was poun—not poun—yeah, I guess pouncing at him and I told him—I said, "I'm not going there just to say things that you want to hear. That's the whole purpose in going. You know—to speak how you really feel," and I told him I was going to mention it to you this week and I told him if he couldn't deal with it—if he couldn't deal with me telling the truth then maybe we all shouldn't go together.

THERAPIST: Isn't that funny, 'cause I looked at the tape and I thought you were pouncing on her, at the end of the session.

FATHER: I—I keep telling, it wasn't—it didn't have that much to do with the session, it's just things I had on my mind. Anytime I'm quiet she takes that as I have a problem.

Comments: Recall that this is part of their repeating sequence of behavior—father gets quiet and mother frames his behavior as indicating a problem.

MOTHER: No. He called me "Miss Perfect"—

FATHER: That was from the session.

MOTHER: —and in the sarcastic way he was saying it and he had an attitude and my son, the whole family noticed it. He had one. He had a visible attitude towards me. He was sullen and then—

BENJI: Daddy had an attitude too.

THERAPIST: Um-hum.

FATHER: I guess I don't see these things. I don't know. I must be coming from a different place. I don't know.

BENJI: Yes you do.

THERAPIST: Well, I wouldn't wonder if things got a little bit stirred up for you here. That you had a few things to think about.

Comments: The family has reported that Benji has been anxious, that the mother and the father have had some "blowups," and that the father "had an attitude" with mother. The therapist finally generalizes all of these family semantic frames by saying that "things got a little stirred" and shifts to a request for further family semantics by suggesting that they "had a few things to think about." As we will see, the father brings up the subject of the mother's family again as an important issue.

FATHER: Yeah, but it was only on one subject. It had to do with my mother-in-law. See I—I was contemplating a lot of things.
MOTHER: Well, now he told me he hated my mother.
FATHER: I didn't say I hated—
MOTHER: You told me—
FATHER: If you're going to say something, say it. If you're going to quote me—
MOTHER: You said, "I can't stand your mother. Don't expect"—What did you say now? I'm trying to remember—if I can remember it verbatim—you said, "I can't stand—don't talk about your mother to me. Don't ever expect us to be friends"—or something like that—"again."
FATHER: I said—
MOTHER: "I don't want to hear nothing about your mother."
FATHER: I said that in order for us to build our relationship from here on out, as sensitive as I am at this particular point, I don't think input from Georgia will help our relationship at this point.
MOTHER: He said that he didn't realize that she hated him so much and I tried to make him understand that she does not hate him. I said—I said, "Now everybody hates poor William. It's back to poor William. She doesn't hate you, it was just what you"—I said, "Now if you were a mother—if you were a mother-in-law or if you had a daughter or son and she had a wife—he had a wife that wasn't doing the responsibilities that she was supposed to do—or even a daughter, you know how hard you'd be on your daughter."
THERAPIST: Now, what's the best thing that you can do to help him when he's feeling down and feeling bad about himself?

Comments: The therapist shifts from elaborating mother's semantics to exploring political action of mother in response to father.

MOTHER: I'm not his mother and I'm not his keeper so I can't help him anymore.

Comments: This response is mother's proposal for a change in family semantics—recall how previous sessions, particularly Session 1, used the theme that their family consists of a mother and three children.

FATHER: To be left alone and let me work myself out.

MOTHER: But he pounces at me.

FATHER: I don't need any input. The best thing— See, when I'm quiet, I'm thinking about things, I'm thinking—

THERAPIST: Um-hum. Yeah, but she gets worried. When you get quiet and start thinking about things she gets worried and then the best thing she can do is to really start you a little bit, then a little shove will get you a little feisty and moving again. Hmm?

Comments: The father is pointing toward mother framing his silence as an indication that he has a problem—presumably "depression" given the previous background information. The therapist joins with this view and positively connotes mother's responses as efforts to get him started. The father accepts this semantic reframing of their habitual political sequence. The couple is moving in the direction of altering their habitual sequence of interaction, rather than focusing on any particular simple action.

FATHER: Yeah. Could be.

THERAPIST: So the best thing to do would be to start—

FATHER: Communicating—

THERAPIST: Well, start a little—yeah, picking at you a little bit so you'll fight back. Hmm?

FATHER: That could be. I have a lot of things to think about.

THERAPIST: Yeah, I bet you have—

FATHER: I really do.

THERAPIST: What were you thinking about when you left here?

FATHER: In—in a sense I was—I was "Poor William." In a sense I was, when I first left. And at this stage of my life and in putting something together I just don't—you know—it's—it's hard—coming back for—for—a legitimate comeback, okay? I have a lot of things to think about and a lot of things to try to change, 'cause in order for me to change I really have to change. In order for me to make a goal I have to change just about my whole basic makeup and I get angry at times, your know, because—

THERAPIST: Well, but what you want to be sure not to change is this family too much. Hmm?

Comments: The father's strong articulation of "change" is countered by the therapist's request for family stability. This response follows from a cybernetic view that depicts troubled family systems as requesting both change and stability (see the Theoretical Maps section of this book). More specifically, a troubled system requests a change in the way it maintains stability. A therapist must therefore acknowledge and prescribe both change and stability. Sole attention to change will result in the family's demanding that it stay stable and vice versa—strict attention to stability results in the family's demanding change. Therapeutic interventions, from this perspective, require successfully handling the complementarity of change and stability. In the previous session, the therapeutic foundation of "expectations" and "disappointments" provided a way of indirectly addressing change and stability, respectively. In addition, we demonstrated how the positive and negative consequences of father's rebellion also addressed stability and change, respectively. As the present session continues we will see how the therapist more explicitly handles the multiple communications of change and stability.

FATHER: Well, family—yeah, of course, that's what's important.

THERAPIST: Okay. So that's what we want to be sure that we keep the same.

FATHER: Yeah, that's one thing I want to keep—

THERAPIST: So, that's dangerous. When we begin to think in terms of change, then there's a risk involved.

Comments: The therapist uses this opportunity to begin constructing the view that change has its consequences—sometimes including threatening the stability of the more encompassing system(s).

FATHER: Always risk involved in change.

THERAPIST: Right. Um-hum. So we have to be careful not to move too fast.

FATHER: Definitely.

THERAPIST: Did we get a little bit too fast last week?

Comments: The complementarity of stability/change is addressed: by asking the family if they went too fast, it is implied that change will occur with a respect for stability.

FATHER: No.

THERAPIST: Did I lay a little bit too much on you?

FATHER: I don't think so. I could take a lot. I mean—I've been taking—I've been dumping stuff on myself for centuries so—it's just that that one particular night it struck a chord and the chord is Georgia, so I just get upset about that. Until I prove myself, I don't feel that I want to see or hear anything from that part of town. That's just my—my—that's the way I feel. When I do something, then it's fine.

THERAPIST: Yeah, I guess maybe you think Lily wants you to prove something to her mother?

Comments: The therapist is recycling the semantic frame built in Session 2—that of "high expectations." This time she addresses the frame in terms of "proving something."

MOTHER: No. I don't want him to prove something to her.

FATHER: No. Lily, I'm the one—she asked me the question. My name is William. Okay? She directed a question to me. I don't think she—she wasn't involved in this. This is between myself and my mother-in-law. She's a good person and she has a lot of good qualities and it's just that I let—I got a little upset and I want to just come back so it's no more flak on my part. You know, "Tommy did this or William did that and he's not doing his thing" and I'm just tired—that's why I'm making a change, because I'm just fed up with the whole situation and getting dumped on, but I caused it.

THERAPIST: Let me see if I understand. It's like the first change that you're thinking about making is in some way to help Lily get free of her mother.

Comments: The therapist politically places William in the position of helping his wife "get free of her mother." This switch positively connotes his communication about his mother-in-law and implicitly points to the consequences of change for the whole family.

FATHER: Oh. I guess—actually, in the long run, yeah. I guess so.

THERAPIST: Really.

FATHER: Sure. She controls all the way from Georgia. She's a very, very powerful, possessive person.

THERAPIST: Yeah. Oh, yeah. I remember Lily last week telling me how she still feels controlled by her and still tries so hard to please her.

MOTHER: Still, I wasn't that controlled by her.

THERAPIST: Hmm?

MOTHER: I said I wasn't that controlled by her. I married him and she didn't want me to marry him.

THERAPIST: Oh, you have your little rebellions too, I know, but it still matters to you a lot what she thinks and I guess what I'm hearing William say is that maybe he's a little bit trying to rescue you a little bit from that.

> *Comments:* Semantically speaking, the family has now been framed as the father rebelling against his wife, and the mother rebelling against her mother. This implies that both the mother and the father are acting as children in relation to someone and are thus on the same political level.

MOTHER: But he can't rescue me, 'cause I'm not a child anymore. See my mother has—

THERAPIST: That's true, but he can try.

MOTHER: —influence over me, but I also have opened my eyes up and I have also seen that he has not been acting maturely all these years. I've been making excuses for him, because I have been so rebellious to my mother that I was determined that she wasn't going to prove me wrong, but in fact, I—I didn't have any insight to what actually was going on. Like times when he quit his job and didn't work, because he wanted to go pursue something else that wasn't a steady paycheck and he had a family. I went along with that whereas—I mean—that was irresponsible. And this is what I'm saying now. My mother doesn't have anything to do with my really basic decisions now, because I'm grown and I can see right from wrong for myself, now. I think that's what bothers him. I don't need her to tell me what my situation is. I know what my situation is. You know? I know what has to be done. It's just that she—she's a reinforcement. Maybe he doesn't want that reinforcement. I never had that reinforcement from her before.

THERAPIST: Okay. So when you left here, you had a little fight?

> *Comments:* The family's responses indicate that they generally accept the therapist's semantic frames involving rebelliousness and mother-child relations as a way of talking about their situation. Having achieved this acceptance, the therapist turns to recent politics: their fighting.

MOTHER: Well, he picked with him, because when I left—when I walked out I felt this way, I've been in therapy before. I felt it's time for communication. You don't hold a grudge, because what's the sense in having therapy if you can't talk the truth? If you go there and just tell a lie?

THERAPIST: Yeah, but the truth often hurts, doesn't it?

MOTHER: Well, he said some horrible—well, not horrible, but he said some things to me last week and I didn't get all—I didn't get my head all bent out—I mean—'cause I can deal with the truth. He has a way of saying it so harshly, "Miss Perfect," and I know it's not a compliment. I know it's the biggest put-down. He calls me a neurotic. I didn't put a dish away Saturday, so he made a big deal about it, so then I sat down and told him all the things that he did wrong and then all of a sudden he just blew up at me and he—Little Tommy even had to laugh at that situation, it's so ridiculous.

FATHER: Well, as I say I'll take whatever you say as correct, 'cause I really don't—

THERAPIST: Aha. I thought the "Miss Perfect" was Grandma. She was the "super lady" wasn't she?

Comments: By mentioning the term "super lady," the therapist organizes information to connect with the therapeutic foundation previously built.

FATHER: She was a super lady, but she wasn't perfect.

THERAPIST: She was just a super lady.

FATHER: She was a super lady, she had her faults and she didn't—she didn't expect anything that a person couldn't do. You know, limitations—everybody has limitations. She was a good lady.

MOTHER: Why are you laughing, Tommy? You must have a reason for laughing.

TOMMY: It's like my friends talking, but you're in your 30s, not 13s. You know what I mean?

THERAPIST: You mean the quibbling that they're doing?

FATHER: Very interesting. We've got a problem.

THERAPIST: Yeah, well—um-hum. So then you had a couple of little spats? Big ones? Little ones? Like the old ones? What?

FATHER: Short and sweet. Hit and run. It wasn't—it didn't build, you know.

MOTHER: It struck a chord in me.

THERAPIST: It did.

BENJI: It struck my chord too.

MOTHER: It lasted for a couple of days. I felt animosity for a couple of days.

THERAPIST: What, the "Miss Perfect"?

MOTHER: The way he puts me down. The way he tries to make me look bad. I—this is how I feel what he's doing to me—how he's looking for things to make me look—I know I'm not perfect, but he looks for things that make me look bad and I don't understand why.

Comments: The father's rebelling against the mother has changed from "drinking behavior" to criticism.

FATHER: Want me to explain myself on that? I'll explain myself simply. When I create a situation—'cause I create it—it's not as a put-down and it's not as a—it's just to let everybody know everybody is human. You know? I'm not saying to her, "Gee, Lily, you didn't"—I'm not really digging into a situation or I'm not causing a big fight. All—simply I'm trying to say is see, anybody can forget to do something. That doesn't make them a bad person. That's all I was trying to say. Believe me. That's all I was trying to say, but I don't get that, I get a vicious attack that I'm trying to attack somebody. Simply if it was my sons, I show—if they're doing something that's wrong towards somebody I'll make an example out of it and we'll sit down and talk about it, but I guess it's been so many years that she's felt that I've been attacking her, that everything is an attack at this particular point. So, I do understand where she's coming from, I suppose.

THERAPIST: I'm not sure I do, but it's beginning to—it's like—you know—do you ever have sort of a glimmer of an idea but you're not quite—it's not quite—not quite jelled. Remember what I said to him last—at the end of the session last week?

Comments: The therapist recycles last week's intervention as a way of stabilizing the therapeutic foundation that was constructed. In addition, it provides a way of seeing what effect it had on the family.

MOTHER: About black women being stronger than black men?

THERAPIST: Um-hum.

MOTHER: Um-hum.

FATHER: That bothered me.

MOTHER: That bothered him.

THERAPIST: I'm sure it did.

FATHER: Yeah, that really bothered me.

THERAPIST: And we said that one way that black men had kind of found to—was to rebel against—

Comments: Everything the family has presented in the beginning of this session has been framed by the therapist in ways that support the therapeutic foundation built in the last session—expectations, rebellion, super ladies, and so forth. Having done this, the therapeutic foundation is maintained and held on to as the compass steering the communication for the rest of the session.

FATHER: That's part of what I was thinking about. See, she had a chance to speak on the subject. I didn't. Maybe—maybe I thought it was—you were discussing the black male and I was the representative of the black male, also my son, and we didn't have any input on it and—umm—but you covered the area—you saturated it pretty well. I really didn't—after you said what—you know—between the two of you, I didn't think that there was much left to say except to show that all of us aren't the same, so my determination to change that image was where it was set from that particular point so I had a lot to think about when I left here, that was on my mind, plus Georgia was on my mind plus my immediate bill situation is on my mind and a lot of other things were on my mind, so I was moodish—I was in a very moodish, temperamental sort of a way when I left here.

THERAPIST: I would expect so. I would have been very surprised if you went out of here not experiencing some—

FATHER: Yeah, but it was a good—it was a good session. A very good session. I enjoy all of the sessions here.

THERAPIST: Well, but then, William, then maybe what—you really did try to change it a little bit by standing up to Lily—and not in the usual way of just sort of passively not doing what she wants, but—

Comments: The therapist addresses the change in the way he rebels.

FATHER: I'd say so.

THERAPIST: Hmm?

FATHER: Yeah. I'd—we had an argument and words were said and my—my traditional way was, okay, whatever you say, but this time I didn't.

THERAPIST: And then go have a drink.

FATHER: Yeah, right. This time I didn't. I said no. No. I stood my ground.

THERAPIST: You did.

MOTHER: But there wasn't any ground to stand, because I didn't—I didn't bother you. I didn't say anything to you—

THERAPIST: Well, it doesn't matter.

MOTHER: —you attacked me.

FATHER: I wasn't talking about that time. We had two—

MOTHER: You attack my mother, you attack me. You might not like her, but she is my mother.

FATHER: I wasn't talking about that time. I was talking about when we were—we were arguing from the room. I was in the living room, we had a discussion, and you said—

MOTHER: I don't remember. All I remember Saturday is when you had made a big deal about the dishes that I had not completed because breakfast was not over with yet.

THERAPIST: Lily, if he gets stronger, does that mean that you're going to have to get weaker?

Comments: A political frame about their complementary relationship is addressed: when one spouse is strong, the other is weak.

MOTHER: No. I feel that—what he does with himself has nothing to do with me, because he's an individual and I'm an individual. Because we're married does not mean that we have to suffocate each other. He's supposed to grow and I'm supposed to grow. We are two separate people.

THERAPIST: Okay. But what happens when it changes and he becomes stronger?

Comments: The consequences of change in terms of shifting complementary positions are being explored. It's important to point out that the recursive relation of stability and change is now spelled out as follows:

stability of complementary relationship/changing roles
(i.e., strong/weak)

With this relation it becomes clear that a change in roles helps only to maintain stability of their relationship. (Note that this definition of change and stability is in terms of a second-order therapeutic reality where interaction and relationship are emphasized.)

MOTHER: Well, good. It would give me a rest. I won't have to worry about paying the bills. I would feel very relieved.

THERAPIST: Um-hum. Yeah. I'm sure you would. On the one hand; on the other hand, is there some sense that in order for him to be able to do that, you have to back down?

MOTHER: No. Because I'm not going to back down.

THERAPIST: Okay. Good for you, because I—you know.

MOTHER: 'Cause I don't see how him getting strong has to do with me at all. It's two separate entities. Him getting strong shouldn't have anything to do with me. When I got strong, it had nothing to do with him.

THERAPIST: Well, I don't know. I'm not so sure, because you're closely tied in with each other.

Comments: The couple's complementarity and connection are again underscored.

FATHER: I'm not so sure either.

MOTHER: But it had nothing to do with him—

FATHER: It had a lot to do with me.

MOTHER: It had to do with me. No. I'm sorry, I have to—I have to greatly tell you that you are wrong about that. When I went into therapy I found out that I had inner strength within myself and I didn't need—

FATHER: How did you—how did you get there?

MOTHER: I got it from Susan, my therapist.

FATHER: I said, how did you get to go to see Susan?

MOTHER: Oh, because you made me go. You dragged me there.

FATHER: So in part—

MOTHER: Just like I told you, if you didn't go to AA, I was leaving. I had told you that for many years to get yourself together.

Comments: The couple provides examples of how their complementary positions have shifted, with one spouse being the identified patient and the other being the one who is responsible for getting professional help.

THERAPIST: Um-hum. Did he actually—have to drag you into therapy?

MOTHER: Well, no, not drag, but he told me to come on and go. He said he was taking me over there. I had just had my son and I had Mother—the doctor told me that I had—what do you call those—"Delayed Mother Blues." He was about four months old.

THERAPIST: "Postpartum Blues."

Comments: The couple's complementarity even includes an oscillating depression. The therapist will allow the mother to define her experience with depression. The political effect of this discussion is that it constructs more evidence supporting the underlying theme of complementarity.

MOTHER: Um-hum. I had them very severely.

THERAPIST: How severely, Lily? Could you—

MOTHER: Umm, I should have been on medication with him, with Benji, because I had a lot of problems before I got pregnant, because he was not a wanted pregnancy. I wanted to have an abortion, so it was problems before I got pregnant with my last child.

THERAPIST: Um-hum. And was it William who didn't want you to do that?

MOTHER: He had promised me certain things and all the "Over the Rainbow"—

FATHER: Tell her—tell her the certain things.

MOTHER: He was going to have a nurse for me, 'cause I was going back to school. I was going to Hunter College. I was going for my bachelor's and I got pregnant. It was not a planned pregnancy. And I was going to abort it and he told me no, he didn't think I should do it, because he was going to turn around and be the best husband and he was going to have a nurse for me, because I didn't have any of the luxuries with the first child. I didn't have anything. Nothing at all and I always said I would never go through that again. Never. And he told me, oh, it will be different this time. It was a bit different because my mother sent me a lot of money when Benji was born. She sent about three hundred dollars and I bought a lot of things and she helped out with—

THERAPIST: Um-hum, but also William was good with the baby. No?

MOTHER: Well, when he first was born—umm—he wasn't in sanitation. He had quit the union again to go out into some other—one of his other dreams. A commodity that didn't have a steady income, and he was there in the morning a little bit. He would set up a bottle sometime, but it was still very depressing. The phone had been cut off. I was completely cut off from the outside. It was a very bad, depressing time for me. Bills were accumulated. He had owed me money personally that it seemed like he was never going to pay me back, so it was a very bleak time. Very bleak.

THERAPIST: Yeah. And you just cried a lot and were very sad or what?

MOTHER: I cried a lot, I was very sad, I was even thinking about committing suicide.

Comments: Each spouse has, at different times, considered suicide—another example of their shifting complementary roles.

THERAPIST: Um-hum. You were talking about it to William and—

FATHER: She had mentioned it at one point.

MOTHER: And I had called my mother one time, I had called my mother one time—

THERAPIST: Oh, you did.

MOTHER: —and my mother had spoke to William about it also. She said that Lily is not talking right—you know—because I had called my mother—

FATHER: Okay. If you called your mother—

THERAPIST: Those are fighting words now.

FATHER: I don't remember—well, I guess she was involved in it. She prompted me to take action. I guess that's the way it happened. I don't recall it being that way, but I guess I don't remember—

MOTHER: And he was drinking at that time also. He had started back—you had started back drinking when Benji was a little baby.

FATHER: No. I wasn't drinking then. I started drinking when I went into construction.

MOTHER: Well, you went into construction when Benji was a baby.

FATHER: Yeah, well, that wasn't when Benji was born.

THERAPIST: Um-hum. So about how old was Benji when you went into therapy?

MOTHER: He was about four months old.

THERAPIST: He was about four months old.

MOTHER: And they put me on medication and—

Comments: Each spouse has even received the same class of solution—medication. This information further supports the underlying interactional view of complementarity.

THERAPIST: And in therapy—

MOTHER: Susan had told me to endure. I'm not going to go into what I went into with her, because that was personal, but she said, "What you have endured—you are a very strong person. You have to stop living your life through other people, especially through your husband. You have to start being your own person and don't be afraid and don't be intimidated by him." And I had also noticed as long as I was a doormat for him and as long as he—as long as my life rotated around him, everything was swell, everything was fine, but as soon as I started getting independent or thinking on my own, things started getting—you know—just— That's when I really started seeing the real him.

THERAPIST: No. Everything wasn't fine.

MOTHER: No. Everything wasn't fine, because I was in a false state.

THERAPIST: It wasn't fine for him either then. It wasn't fine for anybody.

Comments: This might be seen as a message that family politics wasn't successfully managed. In addition it might imply that all the issues in the past have not been fully addressed.

MOTHER: No, because he would have done better for us if it was fine.

THERAPIST: Right. That wasn't fine. That's not the answer, to submit and get bullied and put out, that's not the answer.

MOTHER: I can't live like that.

THERAPIST: But that's not—that doesn't even make things okay, so that's— Right? But there have been some big changes in the family since—hmm?—since Benji was born.

Comments: This can be seen as a request for historical semantic frames about changes in the family. By discussing these past changes, the idea that another change will take place is implied.

MOTHER: Um-hum.

THERAPIST: And that's always—puts things out of kilter.

MOTHER: But I was changing a little bit before Benji was born. We've been like going our separate ways before I got pregnant and we've been having marital problems. You could see there was a distance getting in between us because I was starting to get a little bit more independent. I had gotten my license and I used to drive around, going to school, and I was getting independent because he was getting out of the way— How old were you, then, about eight years old? Seven?

TOMMY: Eight.

MOTHER: And he was just out of the way now. Little Tommy was out of the way.

THERAPIST: Um-hum. (*To father*) What are you brooding about?

> *Comments:* The therapist now demonstrates to the mother another way of approaching the father when he withdraws. Namely, one can simply ask him what he's thinking (or brooding) about, rather than assume that his silence and withdrawal are indications that he has a problem. Note that this demonstration of an alternative response to father's silence and withdrawal takes place during a discussion about family change.

FATHER: Nothing. Just listening. I run things through my head. I try to go back in time—

THERAPIST: What's running through your head?

FATHER: A couple of things she says. I'm—I'm listening— like—I don't know. I just pick up a lot of hostility and I pick up— Well, I've done a lot of things, so I don't expect any differences really, but this change that she goes through, independence and—it was a period where it bothered me because I couldn't adjust to it. Being an alcoholic, I—I haven't grown in so many years and she did grow when she got her head straight after seeing a psychiatrist. I watched her develop and I watched her take hold, but I couldn't do it. 'Cause— I don't know—I guessed drink would be my solution and I watched her mature a great deal. I watched her evolve into a pretty efficient— a very efficient person. Some of it bothered me, because I saw her leaving me in certain—in certain degrees, certain areas, and I tried to combat it the best way I could, but being as flustered as—an alcoholic is—I'm splintered. I'm broken in so many different places. I have a feeling for ten thousand different—you know—pieces of me and to put it all back together to get one feeling takes a while, so I didn't know if I had that much time. So what I do is I create a situation to slow down the progress of change. I would—when I see that change—if it's a positive change, well, okay, everybody—that's one thing. But her change is a change for her, period. Not for anybody else, and that change breaks to the right. Away. Okay? And I'm trying to keep it straight down the line. And so I did a lot of childish things. I did a lot of immature things, but I did the only—combated the only way I could do it at that particular time.

> *Comments:* The father is providing an example of the type of complementarity earlier suggested by the therapist: if one spouse becomes strong, the other becomes weak. This time, however, the roles are reversed: the father becomes weaker as the mother becomes stronger. The father also implies that change of one individual may threaten the stability of the whole family system and adds the idea that his problem behavior provided a political contribution to maintaining family stability by slowing down the mother's change.

THERAPIST: Um-hum. To try to slow it down as best you could.

FATHER: Try—yeah, slow it down, but then again to make it focus on a positive change and not so much of a change to the left. When I say the "left" I mean—I mean the change that'll benefit everybody in the family, not just herself.

THERAPIST: Um-hum. The thing is that the change was not really a change. I mean it seems like a big change.

> *Comments:* The complementarity of stability and change is reintroduced. In particular, a change by one person is corrected by another person as a way of keeping the family the same. Thus, individual change is not necessarily a family change.

FATHER: To me.

THERAPIST: Lily is much more assertive, but change in terms of in the relationship was not really much of a change, was it?

> *Comments:* The therapist more carefully spells out the logical typing of change, distinguishing change of an individual as distinct from change of a relationship system. Again, change in one spouse is being linked to maintenance of relationship stability.

FATHER: Well, not—I don't know.

THERAPIST: Well, she hasn't become more accepting of you. She hasn't nagged you less, she hasn't really supported you more.

Comments: The therapist is demonstrating how Lily's individual change didn't change the relationship.

FATHER: No. No. No. The more assertive she became, the more hostile she became.

THERAPIST: Yeah, but that was always so.

FATHER: No. No.

THERAPIST: No?

MOTHER: Oh, when I was his doormat I wasn't hostile at all.

THERAPIST: No? Really?

MOTHER: No. He was my—he was my whole life. The whole world rotated around him, because he manipulated me very well.

THERAPIST: You mean you were a happy doormat?

MOTHER: I wasn't really happy—

FATHER: She wasn't really happy.

MOTHER: —I held—I contained it inside.

Comments: This can also be seen as supporting the view of complementarity—recall how father has described himself as withdrawn and inside himself in relation to mother's efforts to help him.

THERAPIST: You contained it, but you must have—you must have let him know in some way. That generally comes out—

FATHER: She let me know at times.

MOTHER: At times.

THERAPIST: —you can't be a doormat without feeling very bitter.

MOTHER: But he had me very well manipulated. He had me believing—you know—I believed all his stories, you know? I guess 'cause I wanted to, put it that way. I guess I wanted to be a doormat— I don't know. Some sort of inadequacies within myself.

THERAPIST: Yeah. I'm just—I guess what I'm saying is that the change isn't as big as it seems.

MOTHER: But for me it seems big, because I—I—maybe if I started a relationship with a new man it wouldn't be that big, but having an old relationship—having a relationship with a person that you lived with and then you changed it, it seems—maybe it seems bigger than what it is because he tells me it's big.

THERAPIST: See, when I say that it isn't so big, because you really haven't stopped expecting much of him. It isn't as though you're counting on yourself to do what you want to do and can let him be. You still are very much hooked in, into his changes and what you want from him. That hasn't changed.

Comments: The therapist again demonstrates that individual change does not necessarily mean change in the relationship, this time using the foundational theme of expectations.

MOTHER: It's changed somewhat, but not drastically.
THERAPIST: Right?
FATHER: I guess so and then again I don't—I think she's— she's—become more focused on what she expects now. Before it was hit or miss, you know? Now it's definitely focused on what she wants and what she expects.
THERAPIST: Really?
FATHER: Yeah, yeah.
THERAPIST: What does she want from you?

Comments: As the mother and father continue to define change on the level of individual change, the therapist will challenge them by saying that change has not occurred on the big level, that is, the level of their relationship. Thus, when mother and father propose that the mother has changed, the therapist simply counters them with a question about their relationship, such as "What does she want from you?" This question requires that they jump to the level of relationship from which they can more easily see whether change at this level has convincingly occurred.

FATHER: She just wants me to handle my responsibilities. That was before. Now it's more—it's become more materialistic. Things that she wants out of life that she thinks she—
THERAPIST: She's much clearer. Hmm?
FATHER:—deserves. And, yeah, she's a lot more precise about what she wants and—
THERAPIST: And she feels freer to ask for it.
FATHER: Yeah. In other words, if you can't do it, then I'll have to get somebody else who can.

Comments: Note that the parents still discuss change from the perspective of each individual.

MOTHER: I never said I would get somebody else who can, I said—

FATHER: I speak my—I'm speaking feelings. You never said that.

MOTHER: —I told—I told—I told you that I could do bad by myself. That's what I told you.

FATHER: Correct.

THERAPIST: You could do what?

MOTHER: I could do bad by myself.

THERAPIST: You could do bad by yourself. Yeah. I was looking—as I say I always look at the tape—you know—and I was—it's almost like I could hear your mother's voice which says—you know—the lesson that she taught you or tried to teach you, I'm not sure she managed to, was that you cut your losses and get on with your life. Something doesn't work out, you cut your losses. Her family didn't work out for her—her folks, and she just cut off and went up—William didn't work out, so she cut him off.

> *Comments:* The therapist introduces meaningful noise in terms of a historical semantic frame that embodies political patterns somewhat isomorphic to the couple's interaction. In other words, the therapist is making her point about different levels of change from a broader perspective. Communicating that Lily sounds like her mother also implies that there has been no change across generations—mother and daughter are basically the same. With this message, Lily's individual change not only implies stability of her relationship with her husband, but includes stability across generational lines.

MOTHER: She's like that.

THERAPIST: She is like that, hmm?

MOTHER: And I guess she feels that I procrastinated with him and—you know—just took me—there's just so much suffering anyone can take, unless you enjoy it—you know—but then when I tell her—

THERAPIST: Um-hum. Well, but there are other ways. You don't have to cut your losses and run. There must be other ways of changing things. No?

Comments: This is a request for an alternative way of changing the way she changes in order to achieve relationship stability.

MOTHER: But after a certain time you have to know when you have—when—when you can walk around that brick wall and not try to go through it and I think after—I've been married to him now, fourteen years—I mean—I know a lot of my friends that wouldn't give a man a year if he didn't do right. Believe me. That's how assertive they are. They don't feel that they're a doormat for anybody. They have very good self-esteem. I mean—you have to start saying, well, gee, maybe I like this kind of treatment—you know—I'm not doing anything about it, 'cause if I did, something would have been done already.

THERAPIST: We talked about William's rebellious streak a little bit. What shape does yours take?

Comments: The therapist channels the mother's discussion of assertion toward the theme that had been built earlier—rebelliousness. This is another clear example of how the therapist organizes information: all communication by the family is steered toward maintaining the therapeutic reality previously constructed.

MOTHER: What do you mean? *(Laughing.)*
THERAPIST: You're a bit of a rebel too, you know?
MOTHER: I am.
THERAPIST: See, I know what shape his takes fairly well, you nag him, or you get on him—

Comments: By mentioning father's rebellion, the couple's shifting roles and complementarity are again underscored.

MOTHER: I don't know what shape mine takes.
THERAPIST: "That little click," he said, "that goes on that says, I'm not going to do that, she's not going to get me that way." Right?
FATHER: Correct.
THERAPIST: Yeah. Right?
MOTHER: I don't know which—which—maybe my rebellious—maybe my rebelliousness towards him was to delete him and get him out of my life. That's a form of rebellion.
FATHER: Almost did, two summers ago.

THERAPIST: Two summers ago she almost left you?

FATHER: Yup. Two summers ago. She just was a whole different person.

MOTHER: He was drinking very heavily and that's the summer he choked me—almost choked me to death in the kitchen.

THERAPIST: Um-hum. That was when that fight occurred. Um-hum. But you didn't leave him.

MOTHER: No. I guess because financially I kept saying I wasn't ready and I guess I was looking for excuses.

THERAPIST: So what form does her rebellion take?

FATHER: Now? It changes. Now it's—now it's more. Like I say, it's just like going to college she's—she's ready to get her degree. She's getting very precise. Very—I don't know how to explain it—how can I possibly explain it? Before, she never used to hurt me knowingly or, let's just say, abandonedly, now it's whatever, whatever—the dishes aren't done—this—this—whatever. A lot of things now. It used to be something—it had to be a pretty big situation for her to come in and say, "Well, you didn't do this" and become very ambivalent, but now it could be any reason. Could be anything. I'm an alcoholic so I give her so many—so much ammunition.

THERAPIST: You're not drinking now, are you?

FATHER: No.

MOTHER: I'm so tired of hearing about your alcoholism.

Comments: The mother is rebelling against the father in the session.

THERAPIST: You're not drinking now.

FATHER: I'm not.

MOTHER: He—you know—he uses that as a crutch. I was reading the *Globe* last week, where this little black child was cut off from his—from his—um—he doesn't even have a—he's wearing a bag—an intestinal bag where he has his—where he goes to the bathroom. Where he urinates. And this child is happy and he's—he told—he told the reporter that he was not handicapped. He—what did I tell you? What did his mom say he could do, play baseball?

FATHER: Football.

MOTHER: Football. He's trying to do everything. He doesn't want his mother to help him and all he throws at me all the time. "I'm an alcoholic. I'm an alcoholic. I'm an alcoholic, I'm an alcoholic, I'm an alcoholic, I'm an alcoholic." And I just feel that that's another way of him throwing his weaknesses at me. To tell me, "Well I've got a reason and that's why I'm not doing this and I've got a reason and that's why I'm not doing that." I'm a double minority. I'm a black female and it's tougher for me than it is for him or anybody else to make it in this world.

Comments: The mother's criticism brings forth the political advantages of husband's drinking. She also proposes a competitive posture by saying she is worse off than her husband.

FATHER: That's not so.
MOTHER: Well, that's how I feel, that I'm a minority.
FATHER: I know that's how you feel.
MOTHER: And I feel this way, if—if I don't have self-pity for myself then why—who gives you years and years and years of—to have self-pity. Why should the world stop for you? The world doesn't stop for me or anybody else.
FATHER: Correct.
MOTHER: I've had a lot of tragedies. He's had a pretty cream-puff adolescence and childhood compared to mine.
FATHER: Well, you've had a lot of—you've had a couple of experiences.

Comments: Some observers might propose that the couple's complementarity, which involves shifting role positions, is itself part of an underlying symmetrical competition over whose life is worse. On one level, that of complementarity, they cooperate in letting each other have a round at being symptomatic. At another level, they compete as to who is winning the game of having the worse life.

THERAPIST: No. Well, I'd say—as I say, neither one of you had great luck.
MOTHER: That's why my mother never wanted us to marry, because she said that both of us had previous lives that were not stable and that she said I should have married someone that had a more stable, normal childhood than a rocky one like mine. I guess she foresaw that. And she was right.
FATHER: Well, she did say that, she did say that.
THERAPIST: Every time she quotes her mother you get your— you get a little bit hot under the collar.

Comments: The therapist addresses the father's response as a way of steering the session to focus on rebellion.

FATHER: I don't mind her saying something, but talking through other people just turns me off. You know?

MOTHER: Well, I'm sorry. Other people is not my—you know—we better cut this conversation, because I'm getting a little aggravated with you now—

FATHER: There's nothing to get aggravated about.

MOTHER: Other people is not my mother.

FATHER: I'm just explaining how I feel.

MOTHER: If your mother was alive today you'd feel the same way. I wouldn't talk about your mother like that.

FATHER: Lily, I'm not talking about your mother, dear. All I said was—

MOTHER: Listen, he finds ways of getting underneath my skin.

FATHER: How could I get underneath your skin when I'm expressing my feelings?

THERAPIST: It's like—you know—it's an interesting thing how loyalty in the family is such a powerful thing. I remember when my kids were little. I remember I had a son and a little daughter and the baby was in the carriage and I came downstairs to find him fighting with some kids, but I mean really creaming this kid, he must have been this big, and he said to me, "Nobody"—he said, "Nobody can spit at my sister but me." (*Laughter.*)

Comments: The therapist contextualizes the couple's argument as related to "family loyalty." This semantic frame carries with it the implication that their present political impasses are rooted in a broader social context of intergenerational process. One political effect of this view is that it invalidates any logic for either spouse blaming the other.

FATHER: Strong feelings.

THERAPIST: Right?

FATHER: Very strong. Very strong.

THERAPIST: That's the way Lily feels about her mother, right? It's okay if she is angry with her. It's okay if she's hurt. It's okay—

MOTHER: That's right. And it is all right. It is okay.

THERAPIST: I understand. That's loyalty.

Comments: The theme of loyalty is underscored again. These exchanges are another example of how the therapist has channeled the couple's communication to establish and maintain a particular therapeutic reality—in this case, the themes of "rebellion" and "family loyalty."

MOTHER: But he takes a lot of pot shots at her—you know—and in the past I used to say, "Okay, well I—I used to—I didn't feel that good about myself, so I used to let him say whatever he said about my family, but now I don't feel that way. I feel good about myself and I feel good about my family. They're not perfect but they're still my family.

FATHER: They're not perfect. You can say it.

MOTHER: They're not perfect, that's right.

FATHER: They're not perfect, but they're still my family.

MOTHER: That's right.

FATHER: But your husband's not perfect, but he's shaky about being your husband.

MOTHER: You totally "F'd"up. No. There's a difference between not being perfect and just being an ass. I'm sorry. There's a big difference of being irresponsible, reckless, noncaring, and destructive to yourself and anything around you—

FATHER: Then it goes back to—

MOTHER: When you have weeds in a flower garden you eradicate it.

FATHER: That's a good philosophy.

MOTHER: Now there's a difference between you and being—and not being perfect. Little Tommy is not perfect. He's not going around destructing, destroying everything that comes in his path.

FATHER: That's true.

MOTHER: I'm not perfect, but you—no, you had a severe problem when you just up and quit your job, and my children didn't even have a Christmas tree? Two weeks before Christmas you quit your job, because you wanted to go into construction? No.

THERAPIST: Tell me about the construction business a little bit.

Comments: This question helps calibrate the couple's argument. Note, however, that the couple's argument could be framed as connected to the themes of rebelliousness and family loyalty, thus contributing to the previously proposed therapeutic reality.

FATHER: No.

THERAPIST: No, so what—what—

FATHER: Manage.

THERAPIST: What? A crew?

FATHER: That was—yeah— that was another episode of—I don't know. I had compulsions and most of the time they dictated what I wanted to do.

MOTHER: Can I say to you at this time also the same mother-in-law that he's talking about has lent us $3,800. Has lent us $1,500, because he didn't have money to pay the bills. He didn't have money to pay the rent. The rent was backed up three and four months. Okay? So these are reasons why I feel the way I do and my mother has kept quiet about this situation for a long time. There comes a breaking point for anybody.

FATHER: I never said it didn't.

MOTHER: There comes a breaking point for anybody.

FATHER: I never said it didn't, Lily. I still have feelings and my feelings don't change.

MOTHER: Well, I still have feelings too and my feelings don't change. I was the one that had to call and beg for that money. Do you know how that—Do you know what that took for me to have to ask my mother for that money?

THERAPIST: When he went into the construction thing, was that sort of something that he talked to you about before or he just came in and announced that—

Comments: This question approaches the mother's political involvement with her husband in his business deals.

MOTHER: No. He told me—he was—he came home and told me he was quitting his job. I said,"William, you got to be crazy." "I'm doing what I want to do and I'm not letting you or this family or nobody else stop me from doing it." I said, "Tommy, it's two weeks before Christmas, how are you going to tell me that you're going to quit your job. What about these bills?" "I'll find a way, my unemployment." I said, "Unemployment?" Is that what happened?

FATHER: That's what happened.

MOTHER: He didn't get laid off, he quit that job and he was making a—he was in his union making $450, $500 a week, and he quit it for a year, one solid year.

THERAPIST: Um-hum. What went into that? What were you thinking?

FATHER: I didn't like it. I wanted to change, but I didn't do it— I didn't structure it correctly, of course. I never did anything the right way. I did it my way, and my way is never right.

Comments: The themes of "high expectations" and "disappointment" reappear.

THERAPIST: Well, because it didn't turn out. If it had turned out and you were rich today, then it would have been the right way. Right?

FATHER: It would have been fine. I—yeah. Correct. Yeah, it just didn't work out.

THERAPIST: We tend to judge things by the results and—but your intention was what?

Comments: The therapist finds a way to positively connote the father's failure by pointing to his intentions.

FATHER: My intentions were honorable, but it wasn't the right thing to do. It wasn't the right thing to do. If I would have thought about it now—you know—if it were to come into play at this time I would have thought it out a lot more clearly. I wouldn't have made that kind of move. I would have did both of them at the same time.

THERAPIST: You mean you would have stayed at your job and tried construction.

FATHER: Sure, and worked at night and any other spare time I could have.

THERAPIST: You a pretty good risk taker?

Comments: The therapist again positively connotes the father's failure by introducing the semantic frame of "good risk taker."

FATHER: I used to be. I used to be, but now—I'll still take a risk, but now not at the expense of my family. Let's put it that way. There's plenty more risks for me to take out there, but it won't be—

MOTHER: You just took risks this summer—

FATHER: Well, I wasn't—

MOTHER: With Sam.

FATHER: That wasn't really a—that wasn't really something I looked for. Something that came to me.

MOTHER: You were out of work from May until September.

FATHER: Yeah, and I could have—I could have got back a lot quicker than I did. Somebody called me up with a proposition to get back involved with construction, because he knew I was in construction and I had experience, and he claimed he had X amount of dollars and it would be a good package and we went as far to put the corporations together and— We had a lot of people involved and they found out that this person's capital was as bogus as he was and again it fell apart. So—this time I'm not depending on anybody but myself for anything I get involved with from here on out.

THERAPIST: Maybe you're depending on Lily to remind you of all your past mistakes, so that you don't get too confident again?

Comments: The therapist positively connotes Lily's nagging about his past mistakes as a way of helping him avoid high expectations that lead to disappointments.

FATHER: No. I'm not going to get confident again.

THERAPIST: You sure?

FATHER: Not to the point— I might pursue something after four o'clock, but I'll never—I'll never—umm—just—as a matter of fact I'm going back to school for training to get back into construction on a steady pay basis. Now that I go to school after I finish work.

Comments: The father reports a change in his behavior.

THERAPIST: You've already started that?

FATHER: I have an interview. One more—a final interview before I can go into—it's a credited course. It's a year and it's $1,500—$1,800 or something like that and I'm going to pursue it, because I like construction and I feel that sanitation is demeaning for my talents. I feel that I'm worth a lot more than that.

THERAPIST: Um-hum. What do you think of that, Lily? His going to school to do that.

MOTHER: I think that he should better himself.

THERAPIST: You do agree with that. You think that that's a worthwhile project.

MOTHER: It's almost inhuman, the way they work.

THERAPIST: I want to ask you a very important question. Whose idea was that, yours or Lily's?

FATHER: Of what, construction?

THERAPIST: Yeah, going back to school to do that.

FATHER: Mine.

THERAPIST: Yeah. One hundred percent yours?

FATHER: She didn't even know anything about it. I already had the classes already picked out. Then I told her over the telephone that's what I intended to do. So—I intended to spend a year in school at night and then another year—instead of—usually I say two weeks. If it was the old me, "Two weeks I'll have a job. Don't worry about nothing. I'll quit sanitation and I'll have a job." This time I'm going to school for a year and I'm going to look for a job for a year, while I still have the job.

Comments: This is a change in the family: the husband has initiated his own goals and plans, independent of Lily's expectations.

THERAPIST: While you're still working. Yeah.

FATHER: And then I'll probably work the two until whichever one is more successful takes a play.

THERAPIST: Um-hum. I guess the only thing that would worry me is if Lily got too encouraging about that.

Comments: This precaution arises from the therapist's definition of their paradoxical relationship that was given in the second session.

FATHER: Too encouraging? Well, she stays out of it.

MOTHER: I stay—I stay right out of it. I have taken a very low profile. We've just started talking really. That's how bad things were between us.

THERAPIST: You know why I think it would be really a big mistake if you got too enthusiastic or too encouraged by that?

MOTHER: Why?

FATHER: Failure.

THERAPIST: Huh?

FATHER: Failure or not to complete something?

THERAPIST: No, no, not because she's worried about your failure, but because that's the old game in which you're sure to—if she gets too invested in that then you're sure to get a little rebellious about it, then you're going to need to turn it over.

Comments: The paradoxical theme of the couple's complementary relationship is again used to point out how the wife's encouragement is not necessarily helpful.

FATHER: It's possible as long as—I don't think it will take any—it will have any input into the family as long as it's not taking money out of the family.

THERAPIST: William, the dilemma for you is always going to be that on the one hand you really are an ambitious and a smart man and you really want to make it, on the one hand. On the other hand you also feel the importance of being your own man, so that when somebody, particularly a woman like your grandmother and your aunts and your wife, begin to want something from you, then you have to prove that you're not going to follow them. That you're going to be your own man and you can't do what they want you to do.

Comments: The therapeutic foundation and intervention constructed in Session 2 is re-articulated: the father rebels against his wife's (and other women's) advice as a way of experiencing his autonomy. The therapist will recycle this semantic frame about family politics over and over again, using what the family presents as particular cases of this pattern. In this way, a higher-order therapeutic reality is maintained.

FATHER: Well—
MOTHER: It makes sense.
THERAPIST: Then you get stuck. Then you get stuck there because you can't then move. Right? And that's a real dilemma because I think you have a lot of drive of your own. But then the minute you pick up that old story of these women in the background that want you to shape up and fly right, that good old rebellious spirit comes charging up again.
FATHER: That makes a lot of sense.
THERAPIST: Then you get very mad at her and you get mad and you figure you will talk about her mother. And the dishes and—
FATHER: Another woman, yeah. I know.
THERAPIST: Another woman who wants you to shape up.
FATHER: Yeah, right.
THERAPIST: And I think it probably really—if you do—if you were to really make it in the world. It probably would make you very angry that it would please her mother.

Comments: The therapist's re-articulation of the paradoxical definition of the couple's situation has extended his rebellion to include other women in his background. This enables the therapist to add his mother-in-law as one of the women he rebels against.

FATHER: I thought about that.

THERAPIST: That would probably really get—

MOTHER: But it wouldn't please my mother no matter what you did right now, so—

THERAPIST: Oh, terrific.

FATHER: I thought about that and then—

MOTHER: That should give you more drive.

FATHER: And then when I thought about that I didn't feel hostile towards her anymore.

THERAPIST: No?

FATHER: No. I figured that she was correct on certain parts and then the anger—I use my—I use her—I use her mother as a catalyst, because she's down on me, so I say, "Well, I have to prove to this lady." See—

THERAPIST: Yeah, but again that's the same bind then, because on the one hand you want to show her. You want to prove she's wrong, but you know then again, remember I spoke about the paradox of it, because on the one hand you want to show her that she was wrong about you then on the other hand you're stuck with doing what she wants you to do.

Comments: This is a recycling of the previous intervention to specifically address his relationship with his mother-in-law.

FATHER: Yeah, but this time it will benefit me. I'm not going to be stubborn. I know I can do it, but I was fighting myself. You can't win a battle if you're fighting yourself. You'll split in two parts, so this time I'm going to unite and stay as one, as myself and I'm going to—I'm going to succeed. It may take me time. Time has been a problem with me, dealing in patience. That's not one of my virtues, but I'm trying to muster some—

THERAPIST: Well, I don't know about time and patience, those are always hard for everybody, but the thing is—

Comments: The therapist organizes information.

FATHER: Especially me. (*Laughs.*)

THERAPIST: —but the thing is, what gets in the way is that the minute somebody starts pushing you, you start backing up.

Comments: This comment shifts his behavior back into the context of social politics rather than psychological traits.

FATHER: That's—that's right.

THERAPIST: So then patience has nothing to do with it.

FATHER: That's absolutely correct, because when a situation comes up like that, I drink.

THERAPIST: Um-hum. (*To Tommy*) How about you, how are you about getting pushed?

Comments: The therapist addresses the sons with the same semantic frame that accounts for father's behavior.

TOMMY: I feel okay being pushed. I don't mind.

THERAPIST: You don't mind.

MOTHER: I think Little Tommy likes for me to push him, because that's some way that I give him attention.

Comments: These responses could be seen as further indications of a coalition between Tommy and his mother against his father.

THERAPIST: Well, in some way he must feel pretty strong himself then.

MOTHER: Oh, he's strong. He has a lot of me in him also. He's a manipulator like his father, but he has—he's a good kid. He's strong.

THERAPIST: Well, we are all manipulators, question is, is it in a good cause?

Comments: Manipulation, implying change of people, should be connected to a so-called "good" cause, such as maintaining a social system's stability.

MOTHER: He's a master at it. He even told me a couple of weeks ago, "Yeah, I got mad 'cause I couldn't manipulate you anymore." He told me that to my face when he got sober one morning. Didn't you?

FATHER: Sure I did.

MOTHER: He said, "I couldn't manipulate you anymore," the time he got—he was drunk and —

THERAPIST: You think—do you think you're really stronger than he is?

Comments: The therapist channels this information to read-dress the couple's complementarity of strength and weakness.

MOTHER: I don't—I don't try to—that's what he tries to do, he tries to match the wits, because he used to tell me, "You're not as strong as I am. You're not even a mere pittance of what I am." And I used to tell him, "I'm measuring my strength against you, I'm just telling you that I'm not weak and you're not going to walk over me."

THERAPIST: Okay. The little guy (Benji) is tired, snoring away. Let him sleep. Let him sleep.

MOTHER: I like strong men. I like strong men, that's the ironic thing about it. I like strong men.

FATHER: I still say and I will say over and over again, that the only reason why we are together is that you do know—see, you know a side of me that other people don't know and you do know that if I ever did put it together I could achieve what I want to achieve. I know that's true.

MOTHER: Some people it takes them until they're fifty.

FATHER: I'm not going to do that.

MOTHER: And I'm just saying I've run out of fuel.

FATHER: That I understand. I'm not saying stay with me because of whatever, I'm just saying why you stayed this long.

MOTHER: Yeah. Well I—I know that you had good ideas—

THERAPIST: It's also because she likes strong men.

Comments: The therapist reintroduces this semantic frame, possibly with the intent of using it later in the session.

FATHER: Yeah.

MOTHER: I do like strong men.

FATHER: Yeah, that's true.

THERAPIST: *(to the father)* And you always do manage to win everything.

MOTHER: Yes he does. He's a great manipulator.

THERAPIST: Well, however he does it. There have got to be other ways to do it. But I mean—

FATHER: There are other ways.

MOTHER: That's true. There's good and bad ways to do it. I see your point now, okay.

FATHER: There are better ways.

THERAPIST: Right? There have got to be other ways.

Comments: The therapist has repeatedly prescribed change. A change that is implied is that there must be a different way for the father to demonstrate his strength other than manipulating himself out of one crisis after another.

MOTHER: We never got put in the street, he always found ways of getting it. How, was one way, but you did get it and I felt like a pawn in the interim, but you still did it.

THERAPIST: See, the dilemma—you know—see the problem for him is pretty clear—you know—we say that on the one hand he has his ambition and his own drive and he really—he really does want to make it in the world for himself, for you, for these beautiful children. On the other hand he's doing it for somebody else. He doesn't feel like he owns it, that he has to do it over, so that's his problem. That's—

MOTHER: Yeah, he always tells me, I'm going to stop drinking for you. I say, "No, no, no babe," I said. "You got to stop drinking for yourself. For you. You got to do it for you. You've got to live for you. You can't live for me and the kids."

THERAPIST: Yeah, but when you tell him, he's no longer doing it for him.

Comments: Their paradoxical relationship is again pointed out.

MOTHER: Yeah. Um-hum.
THERAPIST: Right? Then he's stuck with it. And he can't do it for himself. He's doing it for you, 'cause you told him to do it, just as his father couldn't do it for his mother.

Comments: Whatever the family communicates, the therapist utilizes it to maintain the therapeutic reality.

MOTHER: But I don't want him to do it for me.
THERAPIST: No, I mean he's not going to do it for you.
MOTHER: But he tells me he's going to do it for me.
FATHER: That was the last time. Not this time, I did it for me.
MOTHER: Oh. Okay.
THERAPIST: Now. I'm trying to think, you know—where are you stuck in this situation?
MOTHER: I don't know where I'm stuck, but I am stuck.

Comments: The previous articulation of the family's dilemma has been in terms of its consequences for the father. The mother is now being addressed.

THERAPIST: Um-hum. You also are stuck. And you want a man who stands on his feet and you can respect and look up to, or at least a good partner.

MOTHER: I want a man, I want a man—

THERAPIST: On the other hand—

MOTHER: —that I can—that I can be totally myself and I don't have to worry about him and he can take care of himself and I can take care of myself. I don't want a man doing too much for me because then I don't want him trying to manipulate or possess me. I don't want that anymore. I just want to stand on my own and achieve on my own.

THERAPIST: That's what the dilemma is. That's what the dilemma is, you see.

MOTHER: I don't want anything from that person as long as they don't bother me, bother my little space.

THERAPIST: Exactly. That's what the problem is. See? That's where you're stuck, because in one way—it's like you do want a strong man but you're also afraid of it. Also—

Comments: The mother's dilemma is spelled out as a simultaneous desire for and fear of a strong man. This definition leads to exploring the consequences of father's being strong.

MOTHER: I just don't want anybody to dominate me anymore.

THERAPIST: —yeah, because that's like William who had the strength, right? But he was impossible and was dominating and dictatorial.

MOTHER: Well, in a way he was. In a calm way he was.

THERAPIST: Hmm?

MOTHER: He was—in a very calm way he was. He had a kind of power that was very—he didn't shout, but there are other ways of being manipulative.

THERAPIST: So that's part of the problem for you. That on one hand when William begins to show some strength, you get scared.

MOTHER: Well, I don't know—I don't know if I get scared. I don't know—see, I'm kind of bewitched about that.

THERAPIST: Hmm?

FATHER: We talked about this quite a few times.

MOTHER: I don't—I don't—'cause I want him—I get headaches sometimes—'cause I was on Valium. I get headaches sometimes from all this stress. I don't—I want to be able to do what I want to do now. In a way he's right about that. I want to stop being the one that's raising the children and raising him. I want to be left alone now. I want them to go to him and I just want to be left alone. I want him to be strong, but not towards me. I want him to be strong with them.

FATHER: Separately.

MOTHER: Separate from me. Just leave me alone.

FATHER: Strong enough—well, if I get that strong and you're separate and I'm separate what's the sense of—

MOTHER: Why can't you be separate? See, this is what drives me up the wall. Why do I—what is this—because I live with you I can't be separate?

FATHER: Separate? Explain it to me. Explain "separate."

MOTHER: I want to be my own person—

FATHER: Who's stopping you?

MOTHER: —you be your own person. We are both adults. We are not children.

THERAPIST: You know what's stopping her?

FATHER: What?

THERAPIST: Her caring about you. What she's saying is, I want to stop caring about him so much.

> *Comments:* The therapist introduces the classical semantic frame that positively connotes the mother's behavior as "caring." At this point in the session, the therapist is saying that Lily can't change until she changes her relationship with her husband.

FATHER: Yeah. That's exactly what—see, I read it that way, but then I—I—

THERAPIST: But she can't. Okay? She can't. She'd like to.

FATHER: She would like to. I sense that a lot. Believe me. Loud and clear I sense it.

THERAPIST: She would like to stop caring so much.

FATHER: Yeah, yeah. Definitely.

THERAPIST: Okay? (*To father*) Because that frees one, right?

It frees you to get on with your life. (*To mother*) As long as you care so much you get hooked into whatever is going on with him. I understand that and that's—um-hum. Well, okay. I think we got to slow—take it a little easy. Whatever is going to change is going to change slowly, not too fast.

Comments: The therapist prescribes stability after having focused on change.

FATHER: That's right, for once I understand about change.
THERAPIST: It'll change a little, go back a little. One step forward, one step back.

Comments: Change: "one step forward"; Stability: "one step back."

FATHER: Yeah. I feel that way.
THERAPIST: The only thing is that you've got to be sure all the time that somebody else is not pushing you from behind or pulling you from the front. Now that's never going to work with you.
FATHER: No. You're so right about that, though.
THERAPIST: That includes me, hmm? I'm a woman. I know what a dangerous spot I'm in.

Comments: The therapist introduces the present-state politics of therapy.

FATHER: I don't feel, I don't feel that way. I feel—You're neutral to me. Be it male or female in this situation—
THERAPIST: Well, you're right, because I really don't care if you shape up or don't.

Comments: The therapist structures a relationship with the husband that has no high expectations.

FATHER: Sure, because you don't—your life doesn't change.
THERAPIST: Don't care at all.
MOTHER: She's not involved.
FATHER: She's not involved.
THERAPIST: I've got no stake in it.
FATHER: The last therapist I had, she said the same thing, she said, "Oh, my God. All this ambivalence towards women and I'm your— How are we going to have a relationship?" So I told her the same thing.

THERAPIST: Oh, well, we don't have to have a relationship, you and I.

FATHER: No. Well, I—I—I—I feel if I'm going to have—I'm a warm person except for when I'm drinking and I isolate myself, but as long as—I mean—I like—I like to have a flowing relationship. I don't find anything wrong with that. You seem to be a very nice person and ten years from now when I do succeed somewhere, I'd like to see you and say, "See, I did it." (*Laughter.*) Of course I would like to keep that.

THERAPIST: Particulary as I don't think you're going to do it. Right?

Comments: Having previously positioned herself as possibly in an oppositional relationship with the father, the therapist predicts that the father won't change. If they are, in fact, in an oppositional relationship, it is likely that the father will rebel and thereby change to prove her wrong. If they aren't presently in an oppositional relationship and the father doesn't change, the therapist's successful prediction makes it more likely that he will become oppositional with her and subsequently begin rebelling (and changing). In general, if the paradoxical web is spun tightly, all outcomes contribute to more adaptive change.

FATHER: Well, no, I don't think so. When I look into your eyes and concentrate, I feel you feel that I have the capability, but whether he'll ever straighten out that mess he's got there—

THERAPIST: Right. I think you can, but whether you will or not is up—is your choice.

Comments: Having addressed stability ("I don't think you're going to do it"), the therapist now underscores change ("I think you can") and emphasizes that the outcome is his choice.

FATHER: True.

THERAPIST: Your choice. Okay, now next week is a holiday. I won't be here. The following week is also a holiday, but I will be here and I'm going to open the place, 'cause I don't want to let two weeks go by that I don't see you. So I will come in on the Washington's Birthday, right? So two weeks from today.

FATHER: Okay.

MOTHER: You sure you want to come in on that day? You want to make it on another day?

THERAPIST: Yeah. No. I don't want to wait that long. Okay?

FATHER: They look forward to this day, because they really—

THERAPIST: —then I know I'm doing something wrong.

FATHER: Yes, you— No, I don't think so. I look forward to it too—I don't say too much.

MOTHER: I'll tell you something that he had said. I don't think he'll get mad now, but that day when we came here and Benji had said, "No, he is drinking," he had said when he went back to AA. "Oh, we don't have to go back there again." Remember?

THERAPIST: I shouldn't wonder.

MOTHER: That first week. That I said. "No, no, you don't have to go back, but we will go back."

FATHER: Yeah, I said that, I said that. I said—you said—

MOTHER: You were drinking then.

FATHER: Yeah. Now I'm not going to drink anymore so that—

THERAPIST: So everything's okay, but everything's not okay.

Comments: "Everything's okay" suggests a request for stability, while "everything's not okay" suggests change.

FATHER: Far, far from okay.

THERAPIST: Okay, well, we'll see what happens.

FATHER: I want to come back, I like this session. I get a little, you know—

THERAPIST: Well, I hope you get a little edgy and a little troubled by them—

MOTHER: He was troubled last week.

FATHER: I do.

THERAPIST: —otherwise I know nothing's happening.

Comments: The therapist constructs a frame suggesting that the family's edginess is a sign that things are changing.

MOTHER: I think you touched a couple of chords last week.

THERAPIST: I'm sure I did. I'm sure I did.

MOTHER: No chords, melodies. (*Father laughs.*)

Comments: This is an interesting choice of metaphor. "Chords," having more to do with underlying relationships and configurations of notes, are distinguished from "melodies" which are the progression of individual notes (a melodic line).

FATHER: Yes, you did. Yes, you did.

MOTHER: What time do you want us to come two Mondays from now?

THERAPIST: Five-thirty?

FATHER: Um-hum.

MOTHER: I can get here earlier, if you want.

THERAPIST: Oh, I'd love it. Five o'clock?

MOTHER: I can be here earlier than that, if you want. What time do you want us to come?

FATHER: Oh, you're off then, right?

THERAPIST: Okay, let's see, I think I have a—four o'clock?

MOTHER: Sure.

THERAPIST: Four o'clock is perfect. Then we can all get out early.

FATHER: Then you bring the guys here and I'll come straight over from work. Come on, buddy (directed at Benji, who is still sleeping). We're finished. (*Laughing.*)

THERAPIST: Slept right through the whole show, eh?

MOTHER: Thank you.

FATHER: Yeah, it's been a pleasure.

MOTHER: He feels that you're neutral.

FATHER: Yeah, she is neutral. Arbitrator, basically.

THERAPIST: I'm neutral.

In general, Olga Silverstein's strategy for systemic family therapy includes gathering semantic and political frames of reference; using those frames to construct a foundation for a therapeutic reality; and channeling the family's communication in a way that constructs a view of complementarity and connection in family interaction. For this family, Sessions 1, 2, and 3, respectively, have corresponded with these aspects of therapy.

Weaving complementary connections, the focus of this third session includes more fully addressing the multiple communications of change and stability. These communications are structured as a complementarity in which change is seen as the way in which stability is achieved, while stability is depicted as leading to change. This complementarity, the basis of a cybernetic view (see theoretical introduction), is handled by Silverstein as a means of constructing a higher-order therapeutic reality. As we've seen in this third session, Silverstein works to demonstrate how all family communications fit into more encompassing patterns of interaction and complementarity. These complementary patterns may be directly articulated in terms of change and stability or, in more metaphorical terms, using the language of the family, expectations and disappointments, strength and weakness, rebelliousness and autonomy, or individual and family.

SESSION FOUR

Maintaining a Well-Formed Systemic Therapeutic Reality

THERAPIST: So, what's going on in the Thomas family?

MOTHER: Well, to start off, I have a very bad cold. I feel horrible.

THERAPIST: Do you?

MOTHER: Oh, yeah. Umm—things seem to be improving a little. I don't think too fast 'cause I don't want them to— Why don't you start if off?

Comments: This response may be seen as an indication that the family is changing without risk of stability.

FATHER: No. I want you to start it off.

MOTHER: You start it off.

FATHER: I'm feeling fine. I'm feeling wonderful. Pretty good for—that's because I haven't had a drink in thirty-nine days now. The program seems to be working pretty good.

THERAPIST: Yeah. You're going to the AA meetings.

MOTHER: What do you have to say?

TOMMY: Nothing.

THERAPIST: (*to Benji*) I like what it says. Who's the beast? Is that what it says on your shirt? Beast? Is that what—

BENJI: That's football beast.

THERAPIST: Oh, a football beast. I thought maybe it was a Benji beast. No? who gave you that shirt?

BENJI: Umm—my mother bought it.

THERAPIST: You think she was trying to tell you something?

BENJI: I got new sneakers.

THERAPIST: You got new sneakers.

BENJI: My father was trying to make me buy some new sneakers.

THERAPIST: They're very nice.

BENJI: Thank you.

THERAPIST: You work right through being sick. You went to work today?

MOTHER: Oh yeah, yeah. Yeah. I mean—if I had—if I stayed home because I was sick I would—you know—I don't stay home unless I have a fever and we've had some—some real—not tragedies, but my grandfather had to be admitted into the hospital and we got news that his uncle died and—

THERAPIST: Um-hum. Which uncle is that?

FATHER: My wife's— My grandmother's brother passed away, Uncle Matt.

THERAPIST: Oh, Uncle Matt. I remember you talking about him.

FATHER: Yeah. He was an alcoholic.

MOTHER: His uncle was an alcoholic, yeah.

FATHER: He stopped drinking for twenty years and he died of lung cancer. Kept on smoking cigarettes.

THERAPIST: How old was he?

FATHER: He had to be sixty-five.

THERAPIST: Oh, too young, really.

FATHER: Yeah.

BENJI: Let's see.

THERAPIST: Oh, you're trying to think of something to tell me?

BENJI: I'm tired, I want to go to sleep.

THERAPIST: Um-hum. You went to sleep last time. Right? Do you remember?

FATHER: You sure did.

THERAPIST: You remember you went to sleep last time you were here?

BENJI: Yeah.

MOTHER: Yes. Not yeah, yes. I said yes. You say "yes," you don't say "yeah." His behavior seems to be improving a little bit in school, too.

THERAPIST: Really? So are we all finished? Everything's okay now? We're through?

Comments: The therapist challenges the family to provide a problem or reason (i.e., semantic frame) for their continuing therapy. At this point, the therapist has assumed that therapy is nearly complete. Having constructed a systemic therapeutic reality and maintained it for several sessions, the family continues to report changes within the frame of a respect for stability. In this session the therapist will allow the family to present whatever communication they want, including a re-articulation of previously constructed political and semantic frames, hopes and reservations about the future, and new sources of meaningful noise. If the systemic therapeutic reality has been successfully built and maintained, all of the family's communication will fit and thereby continue to maintain it. The therapist's present job is to allow the family to take over what she has helped start.

The commentary for the rest of the session will gradually taper to a minimum, allowing the reader to practice applying his or her own learning to the clinical material.

FATHER: Everything's not okay, but things are looking up. Benji, please, you've got to take it easy. You gave me a fit all the way up here in the car now. Enough's enough. Things are— They're doing—they're doing well, you know. Almost—almost to the point where I'm a little apprehensive to where—you know—they're a little too good.

THERAPIST: Me too. I get a little scared too. When things begin to look too good too soon I begin to worry about what that's all about. (*To mother*) You too?

Comments: The therapist implicitly acknowledges the importance of stability.

MOTHER: Yeah—Benji please, you want to go look at the toy box over there? Umm—yeah, and since we had that blow-out the last time that we was here, I think that maybe we are a little bit more cautious. I know—you know—

FATHER: Things are pretty wide open now. I mean—I think we got all the laundry just about clean or out—at least out in the open.

MOTHER: It's not clean, but it's out in the open.

FATHER: It's out in the open.

THERAPIST: Yeah. That's all the laundry there was?

Comments: The therapist is inviting them to present other information.

FATHER: Well, just covered just about everything in capsulized version. That's about it. Just little things, but the worst is out.

THERAPIST: (*to Tommy*) What do you think, things look better at home?

TOMMY: Um-hum. They do.

THERAPIST: Yeah? They do.

MOTHER: On what percentage basis? Tell the truth. Don't—don't, you know—don't be afraid to open your mouth up and say what you really feel.

TOMMY: I figure it's about—improved almost eighty percent now.

MOTHER: Eighty percent?

TOMMY: I give eighty percent.

THERAPIST: He's giving you a grade. Aha. Eighty percent.

MOTHER: See, things have improved before, but then they've reversed again. That's why I'm a little—

Comments: The mother suggests change and no change (stability).

THERAPIST: Oh, well, that's going to happen right along, Lily. Things never—you know—doesn't go in a straight line. Things get better, they get a little worse, they get better—so that's not—I'm just wondering how it is for you if they are—I guess what you mean by "better" is that the folks are fighting less. They're a little nicer to each other, are they? How is that for you?

Comments: The therapist connotes the complementarity of stability and change as normal and defines "change" as the parents fighting less.

TOMMY: Better. See, they're not hostile all the time. You can talk to them without them getting tense at you so you—everybody is more comfortable with each other now.

THERAPIST: Yeah? You're a little more comfortable with your dad?

TOMMY: Yeah.

MOTHER: Are you really?

TOMMY: Um-hum.

MOTHER: On what percentage basis?

TOMMY: Sixty percent better than it was before.

MOTHER: When you first came in here?

TOMMY: Yeah.

Comments: This possibly indicates a change in the family coalition structure, where father is now more connected to Tommy.

MOTHER: That was only four weeks ago.

TOMMY: That's a long time between now and then.

THERAPIST: You don't believe it, Lily?

MOTHER: I just feel that anything that happens too fast can be lost with the same amount of—

THERAPIST: Well, we're not finished, don't worry. (*To Tommy*) I mean—I'm just—we're just sort of getting started, because— See, my worry is that if things get better between the two of them that you will get a little edgy. You know why?

> *Comments:* The therapist is beginning to address a political consequence of change in the mother and father's relationship: change in their relationship will result in change in the whole family structure.

TOMMY: Why?

THERAPIST: What that would change? You know what that would change? The change between—if things got better between your mom and dad, what would change would be— Well, you wouldn't be your mother's sort of ally, her pride and joy, her best friend, and all those nice things. Hmm?

> *Comments:* The therapist defines the political consequence of this change: a change in terms of the mom and dad getting closer will result in the son and mother's relationship becoming less close.

TOMMY: It's kind of true.

THERAPIST: Kind of true. Yeah. So what's going to—so you might be missing that a bit. No?

TOMMY: No. Not if it's going to be better for the family.

THERAPIST: Hmm? Not if it's going to be better for the family.

MOTHER: But you did one time break the bed down to get even with me and dad.

FATHER: Um-hum.

THERAPIST: That's in this last special week?

TOMMY: No.

FATHER: About a month before we came.

MOTHER: No. It was not that long ago.

TOMMY: A half, two, three weeks before we came.

MOTHER: About a month and a half ago.

FATHER: Brand new.

THERAPIST: Yeah, well, I don't know what that was about. that was before I got to know you, so I don't know what that was about, but I just want to warn you that if things get more than eighty percent okay you might begin to feel a little lonely. Hmm?

Comments: The family has provided information that indirectly supports the therapist's notion of the political consequence of change. Picking up on this, the therapist reintroduces her definition of the consequence of change, but this time predicts that more change may result in the son beginning "to feel a little lonely."

TOMMY: No.
THERAPIST: Not really? Well, we'll see. I always like to look ahead. See, because every change has both a positive and a negative side. You know? So you have to really see what both ends are— Things change—

Comments: The complementarity of stability and change is underscored in terms of political consequences. For this family, change has been differentiated as change that is too fast and thereby threatening to family stability, and change that moves slowly and respectfully of family stability. The presupposition underlying this therapeutic reality is that the family is changing; it's only a question of whether it's changing too fast.

MOTHER: Well I notice since—I notice that since we stopped arguing as much—see, we're trying—we're trying to talk things out now. We're not—we've had some arguments. We have argued some since we've been here.
FATHER: There was one every night after we left here and then on the weekend we had a couple, so this has been about twelve, but in the last—in the last week—
MOTHER: I don't think we've had twelve arguments, Tommy,—
FATHER: —last week—we've had quite a few.
MOTHER: Have we had twelve arguments, Tommy?

Comments: Tommy might now be seen as in between an argument about his parent's arguments.

FATHER: There have been quite a few since we've been coming here.

MOTHER: I said since we saw her two weeks ago.

FATHER: None, really.

MOTHER: Well, we've had, I think, two arguments.

FATHER: A discussion. That was a basic discussion. It didn't—it wasn't a big thing.

MOTHER: No, you told Little Tommy to get out of the kitchen. That was—that was before we—since we've been here. Wasn't it since we was here, Tommy, when he was mad? It was last weekend wasn't it? Yeah.

FATHER: Get out of the kitchen? I get angry. I get angry every now and then. Because I'm not drinking or coming to therapy doesn't mean I'm going to be even-tempered all the time. You know?

MOTHER: Well, yeah. Okay.

FATHER: True. I agree.

Comments: The couple can be seen as arguing over how much they have changed.

THERAPIST: Um-hum, but there were arguments and then they got settled. Hmm?

MOTHER: Well, see, they don't always get settled. We just be nice to each other. See that's what—that's what I'm— They're really not settled sometimes. We'll just go, okay. Well, I won't step on your toes and you don't step on mine, but then it's like a false niceness. It's not really sitting down and getting to the guts of it and really discussing it, because you don't want to get into an argument. You don't want to—not hurt that person's feelings, because you don't want to—you don't want to have to hide hostility again, because the hostility is very stressful in a household.

THERAPIST: Oh, yes.

MOTHER: It's very stressful.

THERAPIST: Okay. Could you tell me what seems sort of unfinished for you? Is there something specific?

Comments: The therapist requests a semantic frames(s) that can be politically examined, related to other semantic frames and meaningful noise, and finally shaped into maintaining the therapeutic reality that has been previously presented.

MOTHER: Well, he—he still has an underlying—he's—he's been very moody. He said—like the other day he told everybody to stay away from him because he's got a lot of things on his mind and he doesn't want to snap at anybody. So I asked him. I said, "Well, what do you have on your mind now?" And he said he didn't want to discuss it. Just—he just wanted to be left alone and he's been moody and I feel sometimes that he's not being very—I don't believe he's being truthful with me. I think something is on his mind, but he's holding it back. I think because—umm—it's like a false—not like a false sense of security, but it's like—it's as if we're strangers, sometimes. It's like he's afraid to be himself or I'm afraid to be myself so we're being overly nice now. See, before it was a strain and now it's overly nice.

Comments: The mother returns to discussing the problem sequence that has been presented in previous sessions.

THERAPIST: Um-hum. Lily, when he gets moody, William gets moody, what happens with you? You start getting a little nervous?

Comments: The therapist is asking how the wife's description of what she believes is the husband's state of mind is politically connected to the wife's behavior and experience.

MOTHER: Well, not so much—well, yeah, it is a little bit nervousness and then I react.
THERAPIST: How, usually?
MOTHER: I get aggravated because I—
THERAPIST: You ask him what's the matter.
MOTHER: Yeah, because it's like an up and down with him. Up and down, up and down. It's never like a medium where he has one set personality. Sometimes—you know—a lot of times William is up and down, pouty and—
THERAPIST: Yeah, well, what does the moody mean to you? It means that he's somehow—that something is going wrong?

Comments: This request for an explanatory semantic frame points to how mother constructs an interpretation of father's behavior. This construction is sometimes called "mind reading."

MOTHER: Dissatisfaction. That something is going wrong.
THERAPIST: That something is going wrong. That's a sort of message to you that something is going wrong.
MOTHER: And I feel we're going to have—there is going to be another explosion. Something else is going to happen now. Maybe he might fall apart again. That's how I feel.

THERAPIST: Um-hum. And then you start getting a little nervous and you start going after him to find out what it is?

Comments: The therapist returns to examining the political organization of this sequence.

MOTHER: Anxiety. Yes. I do. I guess in a way I do attack.

THERAPIST: Um-hum. Yeah. And then—then, of course, it becomes a fight.

MOTHER: 'Cause he walked away from me—

FATHER: Not anymore.

MOTHER: But you did walk away from me. You walked out of the house.

FATHER: 'Cause I said from now on—it takes two to argue, and you're not going to get me—provoke me into a situation. So I said, I'll be nice about it, I'll just walk away. I don't mean disrespect. I just want to be left alone. See, she—like, she says—she takes my moodiness—I'm—I'm trying to change my life. You know? That's not something that you can just do in a—constantly going all the time. This young man has a lot of questions to ask me. She has a lot of questions to ask me—

MOTHER: I have a lot of questions to ask you?

FATHER: Well, we talk. Don't—don't get hostile. It's not a negative statement.

MOTHER: I'm not getting hostile, but don't say I have a lot of questions to ask you—

FATHER: I'm just saying it's constant—

MOTHER: —I speak with you. I'm supposed to be speaking with you, but sometimes I feel like I'm speaking at you and lately he's been telling me to shut up.

FATHER: No, I just said, don't talk—I'm trying to think.

MOTHER: You told me—you were so rude to me Sunday when we was talking about Michael Jackson you made—you tried to make me feel like an imbecile, like an idiot.

FATHER: I didn't mean to do that.

MOTHER: And you cut—and you did it in front of the kids and I told you, "Don't ever do that to me in front of Little Tommy again." This was just Sunday morning now. We were talking and we were "conversating" and he just—"you talk too much and you rant"—it was the way he said it, just cut me right off like you take somebody's guts and rip them out.

FATHER: I was polite at the beginning.

MOTHER: Excuse me?

FATHER: I said I was polite in the beginning.

MOTHER: You see that's what I am saying—

THERAPIST: You know, Lily, I'm not quite sure that I know what—exactly what happened. So—something about what William was saying made you upset. He said you talked—that you also want— I guess what he was trying to explain, as I understood it, was that life in the family is a very busy place. There isn't much room for—

FATHER: Very busy. There is no room—

MOTHER: You're never home anymore, so what do you mean there's no room?

FATHER: When I'm not home, I'm not contemplating, I'm busy. You know? I'm still functioning. I—I—I'm trying— For the first time in my life I'm trying to find out—I'm not trying to find out why I drank, I'm trying to find out who I am and I don't know who I am. I know my name is William Thomas and I react—I act and I react, but I don't know why. I don't know how I should feel. I don't know why. I don't know how I should feel. I don't know—there are a lot of things I am trying to— Now that I'm sober, I'm trying to figure—

THERAPIST: Okay. But when you're moody, see, Lily needs an explanation from you as to what that's about, otherwise she starts getting nervous and feeling that she ought to do something about it.

Comments: The therapist provides a simple way of disrupting their problem sequence.

FATHER: Well, yeah. Okay.

THERAPIST: Right? And then what happens is she comes after you to try to help you or to find out what it's all about, and then it ends up—it escalates into an argument.

FATHER: Sure. Simple to stop. Sure. Change that.

THERAPIST: But I think maybe—I don't know if you could change that in some way so that she would know that when you're feeling moody it has nothing to do with her or—

Comments: The therapist continues to attempt altering their problem sequence.

FATHER: True. I will just have to relate that to her. I'll just say, "I just want to think. I just need to think." 'Cause a lot of times I have to do a lot of reading. I can't get to it. Just some things that I can't— In order for me to change there are things that I have to do, but I can't seem to get to it and I get frustrated at that point.

THERAPIST: Um-hum. And what—angry at yourself?

FATHER: Yeah. Angry at myself, because in order for me to stop drinking, in order for me to make my life go on smoothly, I can't remain the old person that I was. So I'm trying to change and it takes a lot of thought, but I don't get that much time. You know—I can't say that I don't—

THERAPIST: Well, family is a busy place. It always is. It has to be with the kids.

FATHER: That's right.

THERAPIST: What are you thinking about, Tommy? Did I worry you?

MOTHER: He wouldn't tell you anyway, because he is very introverted.

THERAPIST: Well, he's a thinker. Hmm? You think about things. Um-hum.

Comments: The therapist positively connotes Tommy's behavior. (*Note that this again addresses a shift in how mother mind reads, i.e., semanticizes the behavior of family members.*)

MOTHER: He's the one I worry about, because he doesn't express his feelings. This one will tell you, but when he broke the bed down, I knew something was wrong.

THERAPIST: Um-hum.

MOTHER: At first he said—

THERAPIST: What did you think—what did you think was wrong?

Comments: A request for semantics.

MOTHER: I felt it was anger towards me and his father.

THERAPIST: Um-hum. So then what did you do? How did you handle it?

Comments: A request for politics. (*Note that feedback between political and semantic frames continues to be the therapist's lever for constructing useful information. Family members are asked what something means and then asked a political question about their newly constructed semantic frame—or vice versa.*)

MOTHER: I told him that I was—I asked him what was wrong and then he had—first he had—he didn't tell me the truth. He had told me he had did it by accident. That we had bought him a cheap bedroom set and he was making the bed up and it broke. I said, "Tommy, you'd better give me another story than that now, okay?" And then one day when he and his father had an argument, it was about a couple of days later, he told me the truth. "Yeah, I broke the bed because I was mad with you and dad."

THERAPIST: Um-hum. Did that stop you guys from fighting?

MOTHER: It made me more sensitive to my son, to Tommy, Little Tommy, because I felt, wow—you know—we must really be terrible parents that—you know—that he's feeling this way. And I had made my mind up that I wasn't going to—that I wasn't going to give all my attention to him, but I was going to divert it to Little Tommy. See, then when you start getting along, then you have a habit of giving more attention to your mate than to your child.

THERAPIST: Right. So what do you think about that?

Comments: A request for semantics which will shift to political inquiry after mother responds.

MOTHER: I think I'm going to have to learn to work on that because then I'll start having a problem with them and I notice the past two weeks he hasn't been doing his work. I have to stay on him and I've been insisting that this way—I said, I think he's—I'm looking at it psychologically now, I'm saying, well, he figures that if he annoys me that I'll have to give him attention because he's not doing his work, even if it's screaming it's still sort of attention. It's a sort of attention.

THERAPIST: Um-hum. Are you as tuned in to his moods as you are to William's? I mean, if he looks moody like that, do you worry about that?

Comments: A shift to politics. Note that the therapist and family are working on both the problem sequence of the mother and father as well as the political consequences that arise when the mother and father's relationship improves, particularly as they relate to their first son.

MOTHER: He's quiet, but I—I sometimes can sense if he's—
THERAPIST: That he's unhappy or—
MOTHER: See he's—his father is treacherous. He—when he's moody he's an aggressor, he goes out—he goes out to pick—he picks with people whether he realizes it or not.

THERAPIST: Um-hum.

MOTHER: My son is not—he's not the aggressor type. He's the type that I worry about that could be—sometimes children commit suicide because they—they hold it within. He's laughing, but I'm just saying how I feel sometimes when I'm in deep meditation. He's not the type of child to express it like Benji is. And you never know about depression sometimes.

THERAPIST: Um-hum. Does he appear to you to be depressed?

Comments: The mother "mind reads" her son's silence in the same way that she does her husband's so-called "moodiness."

MOTHER: At times he does. He tried to run away from home last year. Was it last year? It was last year.

THERAPIST: *(to Tommy)* What happened?

TOMMY: It was like living in jail. You couldn't do nothing without them yelling at each other or yelling at you. I couldn't talk, couldn't play, couldn't go outside. It was very boring being to yourself so I couldn't take it anymore. So much stuff boring you that you get tired of it so I walked about three miles to my grandmother's house.

Comments: The son calibrated the mother and father's arguments by leaving home and engaging grandmother. Recall that Session 1 had presented the political frame that Tommy was in between the mother and father's arguments. Now we have several illustrations of how this has taken place—his running away to grandmother as well as his breaking the bed.

THERAPIST: Oh, you went to your grandmother's house.

TOMMY: I stayed there, visited my cousin so they would get a little bit off me. And that was it. Then I came back.

THERAPIST: Um-hum. They came after you, or you left a note, or what?

TOMMY: My grandmother called.

THERAPIST: Oh, your grandmother called.

TOMMY: 'Cause she knew something was wrong when I walked all the way over there, so—she called Mother. They had a little talk. My mother, she came over, talked to me. That was it.

Comments: We have another example of how the political coalitions get organized in this family.

THERAPIST: That was about a year ago. Hmm? Things gotten better for you since then?

TOMMY: Yeah, I don't run away anymore. I phase things out. That's all. Like I tune myself out. So now they can argue and I will—I can see it and I'll be upset about it, but emotionally I just feel it's not my problem, I can't change it, so I just forget about it. He'll get upset and he'll come to me and he'll tell me, "Why are they fighting?" And that's not right and he might cry sometimes and he might get mad at Daddy, so I might just take him outside for a walk, because I don't think it should be right for him to watch them go at it, because when they get into an argument, they really go at it. So, I understand that—

THERAPIST: Then you can help him—

TOMMY: Yeah, so he understand more so he won't be confused about them yelling at each other.

THERAPIST: So what's it going to be like if they stop—really stop fighting and things kind of shape up?

Comments: The political consequences of a change in their relationship is again addressed.

TOMMY: More peaceful. Everybody will be fine with each other now, so I can talk to him without him being mad at Mom and he let out stress on me or vice versa with my mother. We can all talk and have a better relationship.

THERAPIST: Um-hum. So you feel kind of hopeful. Hmm?

TOMMY: Yeah.

THERAPIST: Mother right when she says you don't talk about what's bothering you? You tend to keep things inside and—

TOMMY: Most of the time I don't tell anybody, because I don't feel comfortable telling anybody.

THERAPIST: You got a best friend?

Comments: The therapist broadens the political frame to examine son's social ecology.

TOMMY: I don't have—I don't really depend on having a best friend, I have a whole lot of friends. I never picked anybody to be my best friend because I really haven't found a best friend. A person who I can tell everything to.

THERAPIST: How about a girl? Do you have a girl?

TOMMY: I don't trust girls.

THERAPIST: You don't trust girls.

TOMMY: Not—I might talk to them but—not to mean any offense or anything—

THERAPIST: Okay.

TOMMY: I wouldn't want to tell them anything. I feel better telling a boy something.

THERAPIST: Yeah. But girls you think just talk a lot.

TOMMY: They gossip.

THERAPIST: They gossip. Well, you may be right. Think he's right?

FATHER: Maybe at that age, yeah, but older, it's a different story.

MOTHER: And every time his father gets mad with me he gets mad with the children. They can always tell when he's mad with me because he tells them to get out of the kitchen, don't bother me. He takes it out on them. I always tell him, "Why do you have to take out your frustrations, when you're mad with me, on the children?"

FATHER: That's true, that's just—

MOTHER: He stops Little Tommy from doing—see, he stops the smoothness—the smooth flow of the house sometimes. Okay? 'Cause Little Tommy has certain responsibilities, to sweep the floor and empty the garbage at night. Now, I think it was one day last week he and I had had a spat and Little Tommy had went out there to do his work, and he told Little Tommy to get out of here, get out of here. "I'll do it myself, just get out of my sight and go in the room," or something like that.

FATHER: I said, "Go in the room."

MOTHER: He said it nasty. And then I said to him, "By the way," I said to him, "why do you have to—because you're mad or because we had an argument—why do you have to disrupt the whole household?" I said, "How come Tommy can't do his work now? You're going against my orders. He's supposed to—he has a job to do, he's part of the team. Now you're disrupting his life also, because it's really none of his business if you and me argue, but you're making it his business by letting him know that you're aggravated by telling—by telling him that you can't function tonight because I'm mad. So the whole house is not going to function because I'm mad."

THERAPIST: Um-hum. Well, okay, that's true. Some arguments or most of them belong just between the two of you, right?

Comments: The therapist indirectly suggests the political change of moving Tommy out of the position of being in between mother and father's arguments.

MOTHER: But he involves the whole household.
THERAPIST: Um-hum.
FATHER: I guess—I've got a lot of things to change—
MOTHER: The work doesn't get done and I wake up the next morning and I ask Little Tommy, "Well, how come you didn't do your work?" "Well, Dad told me to get the so-and-so out of the kitchen."
FATHER: Anytime I tell him don't do something, I do the work for him. I don't leave it to be undone. I do it myself. Most of the time I'd rather do dishes myself and if I feel that way—I don't know— Sometimes things just seem to mount up. You understand? And the only way I can hash it out— When my day is completed I go through my day and if I had a day to just—I can't—I don't know how—it's a check and balance, it's like a check-off. And if I don't get a chance to check it off in my mind I get uptight until I get everything out of the way and it's like hard to do—I need space sometimes. I really do. I need a little space and it's hard to have space in a family that needs so much from you and I—I haven't been that kind of father. I'm trying to be. I'm trying to change a lot of things. It's not easy, but I—I'm aware of what has to be changed. Being aware and changing is difficult.
THERAPIST: Okay. I'm just trying to measure in my own head as to—Lily said she's worried about young Tommy, and I'm just trying to measure whether there is in fact something to worry about there. What do you think?

Comments: The therapist requests father's reaction to mother's view of Tommy, which may indicate possible political differences.

FATHER: He's—he's a very— That's his personality. He—umm—he thinks a lot. He's a thinker. He's a planner. A lot of times— He—he likes construction. You can't talk and listen to construction. That's something that—you just do. So a person that's into that type of situation—now sometimes when I feel that he is in—when he's out of the norm I ask him, "What's the matter? Do you have a problem? Do you want to talk about something?" And we talk about it—usually it's a girl or a problem that he wanted to relate to. We talk when I come home from work sometimes.

THERAPIST: You do. Um-hum. That's something you share, the two of you, the love of construction work?

Comments: Recall that the first session indicated that Tommy was possibly in a coalition with the mother against the father. The therapist continues to work in joining the father and son.

FATHER: Yeah. He has the love of construction. His mom likes it too.

THERAPIST: Yeah, do you like—

MOTHER: I think he works with construction to blot out everything else. I think it's some sort of an escape for him.

THERAPIST: Well, that's pretty much with most kids these days. No? Didn't you do that?

MOTHER: Yeah. But not as much as he did. I had friends. He doesn't really have any friends. That's what I worry about.

THERAPIST: I see, you feel he's too solitary.

MOTHER: He does not have a normal out. I mean— He's not a happy child. He doesn't seem to be—he doesn't seem to have a lot of life in him.

Comments: One could hypothesize that the mother's talking about Tommy in the same way she describes her husband may have the effect of joining the father and son. In terms of the therapeutic reality already constructed, the son's behavior could be interpreted as loyalty to his father in the same way that his father's behavior has been depicted as a way of being loyal to his own father.

THERAPIST: Of course, he has a lot of responsibility. He has to come home from school and be with Benji, no?

Comments: Introducing the theme of "responsibility" further connects the son with his father.

MOTHER: Yeah. But it's not for long. I mean—all they have to do is do their homework together. 'Cause he's had—actually I was much stricter on him—I was much more stricter than I am now, and I've taken a lot of responsibilities away from him because I realized for his age—at that time he was twelve, it was too much responsibility. I had really put too much on him.

THERAPIST: Um-hum. So that's changing a bit now too?

MOTHER: Oh, it's changed substantially. When he came back from Los Angeles my mother had a long talk with me and I took the overload off of him.

THERAPIST: When you ran away, which grandmother did you go to?

Comments: The therapist turns to examining the political structure underlining son's running away.

TOMMY: My great-grandmother.

THERAPIST: Oh, your great-grandmother. Whose grandmother's mother?

TOMMY: That's my mother's mother's mother.

MOTHER: Your mother's—yeah.

THERAPIST: Aha, aha. And it's that grandfather who is ill?

MOTHER: My grandfather, his great-grandfather.

THERAPIST: His great-grandfather. How is he now?

MOTHER: Not too well. Not at all.

THERAPIST: He must be getting on in years. How old a man is he?

MOTHER: He's—I think—well, they don't really know. I think he's seventy-five, seventy-six, seventy-seven.

THERAPIST: So you went last weekend to help out.

MOTHER: Oh, I've been—we've been doing that just about every other day.

THERAPIST: Really?

MOTHER: Yeah. 'Cause I was the one that had to hospitalize him. I have a lot of responsibility on me with my family, because my family is what you call— Some of my family live in a subculture and are to some extent ignorant. They don't know how to function in real reality that we deal with as normal people, and he was at the point where he would have been killed if I had not stepped in. In fact two police officers found him on the highway that he had been on. He is in his last stages of senility. He's confused. Very confused most of the time and my family is just—you know—they're just as confused as he is. I get aggravated with them because I'm the youngest. I'm the granddaughter and it seems that my aunts and my uncles cannot function more than my five—my six-year-old son, and my mother's too far away, so it's very difficult for her to just drop everything that she's doing and come here so she bestows that responsibility upon me.

THERAPIST: Um-hum. So how does that information get to you? Do they call you to say we need you or—

Comments: The therapist examines the political structure of intergenerational communication.

MOTHER: Well, my grandmother, she calls me for everything.

THERAPIST: Your grandmother. 'Cause the last time you had sort of given me the impression—I guess maybe I got the wrong impression, that you had sort of had cut them off. You really—

MOTHER: Well, I had cut them off. I had stopped speaking to them for what, about a year and a half? I had stopped speaking to my grandmother for about a year and a half, which I thought was abnormal, but at that time my therapist had told me, "If you need to cut your family off, if it comes to a point where it's either you, your sanity, or your family's sanity, of course you go with your own." So I try and help, but it's just that the defeat is—it's like running into a brick wall—

THERAPIST: But if they need you, you're there. You're a very responsible—

MOTHER: Well, if my grandmother needs me, sure, because she is older and I've been taught—

THERAPIST: Yeah. And you're a very responsible person. So then what happens in the family when you're kind of pulled in another direction, to be responsible there and— What happens to these guys? They get a little—

Comments: The therapist suggests that there are political consequences of mother's involvement in her family of origin.

MOTHER: My family suffers sometimes.

THERAPIST: How do they let you know?

MOTHER: Well, Little Tommy won't let me know, but I know 'cause he goes into the room and he hibernates. He—it's not natural. He just doesn't have anything to say to anybody. He never smiles. It's just like he is a zombie. Benji becomes very anxious and he starts acting up in school. In the house he's just running around like he's senseless. And this one—I let his father—I mean he can function on his own, he's an adult.

FATHER: I can function on my own?

MOTHER: Yeah. You're an adult.

FATHER: I'm—I'm—healthy.

MOTHER: I know—I know, but she's just saying how is all this affecting the household that we live in?

THERAPIST: I said, "How does it feel when she is—when the family is pulling her on the other end and—"

FATHER: We both go. We both go. I take care of the situation. I help out with Grandpa.

MOTHER: When he was drinking two months ago it was really—I felt like I was being ripped apart. That's why I said, "Either I'm going to have therapy or I'm going to have a nervous breakdown because I can't take any more of this stress."

Comments: One could hypothesize that the father's problem drinking had the positive social consequence of providing therapy for his wife.

THERAPIST: Just kind of pulled in all directions. Hmm? But William does help you these days?

MOTHER: Now he does. Yes.

THERAPIST: Now he does. Okay. What's the matter—

MOTHER: He did before, but he was drinking before too.

THERAPIST: (*to father*) You're not getting enough credit for what you do?

Comments: The therapist emphasizes the father's efforts to help his wife help her family.

FATHER: I—I—everybody here is—shouts how bad I am, but when there's an opportunity to hear a little good it doesn't even come out, but I guess that's to be expected.

THERAPIST: Why is that to be expected?

FATHER: Well, that's not my family but I helped. I—I really— I go overboard.

MOTHER: I tell you a lot that I appreciate what you do. You know that? I'm really a little sick and tired of you saying that. You know—really. You want me to get down on my knees and lap your feet. You always wanted that.

FATHER: Of course not.

MOTHER: And I'm not going to do it. If I say to you, "Thanks. Thanks for being there with me" or "Thanks for going to see my grandfather" or "Thanks for doing what you did for my grand-mother." That's not enough? And I have said that to you many times in the past three weeks.

FATHER: Yeah. Yeah. You have. You have said that.

MOTHER: What am I supposed to do now, get on the floor and say, "Allah, I am grateful to you?" What about the things that I did for you?

FATHER: No I didn't— Why do you react—overreact?

MOTHER: I'm not overreacting. It's just that you don't realize what you're saying. It annoys me. I have told you how thankful I was that you did have the feelings and the sensitivity to go with me to the hospital and to help me out emotionally, also.

FATHER: Right.

MOTHER: But now you're—you're—you're inferring to her that—

THERAPIST: No, it was just right here. Right here and now that I noticed it. Umm—

MOTHER: He's the type of person I have to constantly tell him something every minute of the day, otherwise he forgets.

Comments: Notice how different this session is from the first. The couple is now fighting over whether the father gets enough praise for helping his wife. In addition, the therapy continues to expose the shifting roles of the couple's complementarity, where the mother now begins to look more like the identified patient than the father.

FATHER: Who, me?

MOTHER: Yeah, you.

FATHER: I didn't ask for that. I didn't ask for that. I mean— You say he is your grandfather. True, but I care about Pop and I help him a whole lot.

THERAPIST: *(to father)* You know—we are talking about how things are changing and one of the things that I'm noticing change here, right here, is that you're willing to take a little praise rather than blame.

Comments: The therapist uses a different frame for constructing the view that the father has changed.

FATHER: Sure, I deserve it, now.

THERAPIST: The first couple of times all we could do—all you wanted was the blame for everything so—

Comments: Recall the earlier hypothesis that the couple could be seen as competing for who had the worse life. The therapist's present comment indicates a change in that relationship game.

FATHER: Well, I needed it, at that point. (*Laughing*)
THERAPIST: So at least that's a change that I'm—
FATHER: Sure is. I agree. I totally agree. Yes, ma'am.
THERAPIST: You don't need to get all the blame all the time.
FATHER: Right. Right.
THERAPIST: Okay. Now, I'd like to talk to the two of you for a little bit alone. I wonder if Tommy would mind taking Benji down to the waiting room for a little bit. Okay? Would you mind? There are just some things—
(*Children leave room.*)
THERAPIST: There are just some things that I want to have a chance to talk about and can't talk about with the kids here. You had said something, implied several times that you had had an experience in your childhood which was something that you don't want to talk about in front of the boys, but something that—you want to tell me about it?
MOTHER: Umm—I—I don't—I don't—I don't know if I can talk about it tonight. I think—you probably already have an idea of what it—
THERAPIST: I assume. Shall I tell you what I picked up? Was that Hank molested you in some way?

Comments: This is therapeutic deduction.

MOTHER: Um-hum.
THERAPIST: Um-hum. Okay. So you don't really have to tell me anymore about it except I just want to know how much— See the reason I need to know it is really only as it gets into—
MOTHER: Well, it gets into my everyday life. I—it does.

Comments: The therapist constructs the frame that historical information will be viewed in terms of its present political relevance.

THERAPIST: Okay. That's what I really wanted to know.

MOTHER: I'll be truthful about it. It does. That's why I went into therapy with Susan and she— It helped me, I would say, about fifty percent, because at one time it was to the point where my oldest child—I couldn't even allow him to touch me. I had a problem. I felt—you know—

THERAPIST: How old were you at the time, Lily?

MOTHER: I was eleven. Ten—ten and a half, around ten and a half.

Comments: The therapist will now examine the political frames that specify dates: when it happened, when her husband actually knew about it, and when she talked to her husband about it. Note that the content of what happened is ignored.

THERAPIST: When you started going out with William, did you tell him about it? Did you ever talk together about this?

MOTHER: I used to—

FATHER: I sensed something.

THERAPIST: You sensed something.

MOTHER: He knew something tragically had happened to me because I always used to talk around it.

THERAPIST: But you would talk around it, never really—

MOTHER: But he sensed it, though, because he never liked my stepfather. He never trusted him.

FATHER: It was pretty easy to sense, you know? There's— there's care and then there's—there's something a little bit more than care—

THERAPIST: Yeah. Right.

FATHER: —and his resentment for me and every other male that ever came by— It was—it was quite evident if anybody dug into it and I'm very perceptive so I just sit and watch things, you know? I don't talk that much, so I was very polite to him, so it was hard to kick me out. I just sat and I watched and I watched and I put it together.

THERAPIST: You put it together, but you didn't talk with Lily about it?

MOTHER: I didn't actually tell him about that until two years ago.

THERAPIST: He knew and you kind of just kept your—

MOTHER: But I didn't tell him until two years ago.

THERAPIST: Until two years ago.

MOTHER: Actually I kept it to myself all—I couldn't deal with it. It was just as if I had pushed it to the back of my mind. My therapist was the one that had told me to deal with it and she had said that it didn't make me less of a person and it wasn't my fault, 'cause I used to feel that in some way it was my fault.

THERAPIST: Well, surely not. At eleven, it wasn't your fault.

MOTHER: But—see, it's easy for you to say that, but how I felt and my—my—my attitudes towards certain—towards men—

THERAPIST: Did you ever tell your mother?

Comments: The therapist explores the political frame that specifies who knows about the event.

MOTHER: No.

THERAPIST: Never. Not to this day?

MOTHER: I wanted to. I used to sometimes pick the phone up and cry and this is about two years ago, about a year or two ago I had—I had a setback, a real serious setback about a year ago and I almost called—I started hating her again. I had these bouts where I hated her because I feel that—I feel that she knew, but she didn't know. That she didn't want to lose her—I don't know—

THERAPIST: Yeah, well, that she didn't protect you. Hmm?

Comments: The therapist continues to address the politics of the traumatic event.

MOTHER: I guess maybe that's why in some sense of the word I am a bit hard, 'cause I feel that I've been abused. Really abused and I came through it all right. I mean—I could have turned to be a prostitute or a call girl or something and I chose not to be that way. I went towards God, you know. I—I—I had a problem with men. In fact to this day I still have somewhat of a problem, but I'm working it out.

THERAPIST: Um-hum. Do you have a problem with each other sexually?

MOTHER: We did.

THERAPIST: Is that a problem? Hmm?

FATHER: Well, we did, but—

MOTHER: A serious problem sexually.

FATHER: We worked it out.

THERAPIST: Yes? Is it okay now?

FATHER: Yeah, I mean—there are times. I can sense in her when she's—there's a certain—I don't know what you say— We communicate, let's put it that way. I know when that's bothering her—the past is bothering her, 'cause she gets forlorn. She just looks at television. I will say, "Did you see that?" She didn't see it, 'cause she's going back.

> *Comments:* Note that these descriptions of the mother's behavior are similar to how the mother described the father in earlier sessions—she would describe father's withdrawal as indicating a problem such as "depression." The couple's complementarity, with its shifting roles of who has the problem and who is the helper, is again demonstrated.

THERAPIST: She's going back in herself again, hmm?

FATHER: So I don't—I don't hassle her too much. Sometimes—well there are certain things in lovemaking that she kind of gets cold if you do something and I—well, I love her, so I understand.

THERAPIST: You're gentle and you know what those things are.

FATHER: To the best I can, sure. And we work things out. One thing I'll say about us, we—no matter what it is, we work it out. We work it out.

THERAPIST: Um-hum. Um-hum. See, you remember the last time I said to you that there's a dilemma for you about William's changing and his becoming stronger, and that the dilemma is that on the one hand you really want him to reach his potential, you want him to do well in the world. You want him to become a strong man. You want a strong man. On the other hand you're scared to death of it.

> *Comments:* The therapist takes the new information from this session (i.e., meaningful noise) and recycles it through the originally constructed therapeutic reality. She now has a way of more clearly specifying mother's side of the dilemma: her fear of strong men. This theme will now be recycled over and over again to the couple. More specifically, every response of the couple will be used as further evidence of this therapeutic reality. (Note that mother's desire for her husband to reach his potential corresponds with change, while her fear of strong men corresponds with stability.)

MOTHER: See, I don't know because— Yeah, what you're saying makes sense, but then I do—I do want finer things in life and—and I do like that Great American Dream and I am somewhat greedy and ambitious, but I just don't want him to try and strangle me. That's all. I just want to still be able to be myself because all through my life I've always been manipulated or held down—you know—that real me could never come out. I was afraid of it to come out. You know—

THERAPIST: No, I understand that. You fight very hard to—

MOTHER: No, I want him to meet all his expectations, but I don't want his expectations to interfere with mine. That's all.

THERAPIST: Well, that's fair enough, but what I'm saying is that there is going to be and I think may be always some fear of a man who is too strong.

Comments: The therapist emphasizes stability. For example, Lily's fear of strong men is calibrated by William's failures.

MOTHER: Well, that could be possible. Sure.

THERAPIST: Not that that can't be overcome.

Comments: The therapist switches to emphasizing change.

MOTHER: I assess rape with strength. I assess when I got raped being overpowered. Being—maybe that's why I can't stand being locked in a room.

THERAPIST: That's right. Overpowered is the exact word. See, but then you get frightened of being overpowered and so in some ways it's easier if you're with a—in some ways now if you're with a man you don't have to be afraid of.

Comments: The therapist now underscores stability.

MOTHER: Um-hum. Well, that's—that's true, but I'd rather be by myself. I've come to that point. If—if—you know—

THERAPIST: Well, that's not the alternative. You know— that's not a good alternative either, so it's just that I want you to know what the dilemma is for you. That as William gets stronger in himself and feels better about himself and becomes stronger, you may get a little more frightened about it.

Comments: The therapist first connotes mother's particular description of change, which was in terms of her individual behvior, as "not a good alternative," and then points to the level of their marital interaction.

MOTHER: Yeah, yeah—

THERAPIST: Okay. So we need to know that.

MOTHER: The unknown. Sure.

THERAPIST: Right? For you it's particularly so, because for you the fear of being overpowered is tremendous.

MOTHER: I can never never be overpowered again.

THERAPIST: Okay. Good.

MOTHER: 'Cause it's either me or that person. That's how I look at it now.

THERAPIST: Okay, but it doesn't have to be that way between the two of you. See, what I'm saying is that that fear will be there and then in some way you're going to have to get past it.

Comments: The therapist addresses both stability and change—the "fear will be there" (stability) and "in some way you're going to have to get past it" (change).

MOTHER: But I think he's trying to overpower me because he always told me that he was going to make it so that I would have to kiss his feet and he was going to make me be subservient to him, and you know I'm telling the truth too.

FATHER: Sure, that's true, but that was—I was really sick at that point. I mean—I said a lot of things that during— Anytime that I'm drinking you might as well throw it in the garbage because it was garbage. You know? I say a lot of things I don't mean. It was my insecurity.

MOTHER: But you understand what I'm saying, that it was still said, so of course I still—

THERAPIST: Well, when you think about it, in every marriage, Lily, the other person always knows your tender spots. Right? So if you get mad at each other you always know just how to go right for the—

Comments: The therapist normalizes their communication.

MOTHER: That's true.

FATHER: Yeah.

THERAPIST: That's always true. That you know each other so well and that you—so he knows how to—I mean if he really wants to get to you or upset you he knows how to do it and you do with him too. It works both ways, right?

FATHER: That's true.

THERAPIST: And if you want to protect each other, you know how to do that too.

Comments: The therapist constructs a complementarity—knowing how to get at each other also implies knowing how to protect each other.

MOTHER: And I get so angry sometimes because I feel—I feel that I've been mutilated. I say to myself, "How can I love my mother and then hate her so vehemently just as strong as I love her at times too?"

THERAPIST: Um-hum. Yeah. But both of those things are there. Very real.

Comments: The complementarity of love and hate is implied.

MOTHER: Very real.

THERAPIST: Yeah. Both of those feelings are there.

MOTHER: That's why with him—the tragic problems I had with him, I guess there is a God up there because if there wasn't a God up there and I wasn't strong I would have—I would have sunk. I would have drowned. And that's why I had become suicidal—

THERAPIST: Well, you're a fighter.

MOTHER: I had—but no, I had one point in my life I wanted to commit suicide. He used to call me lesbian because I didn't want to have sex with him. 'Cause I had—'cause I used to have episodes where I went in a—this thing where it was just like it happened to me yesterday. I could feel the breath on my neck. I could actually feel—I can't explain it to you 'cause you never had that happen. It's just that it was very real to me and then by him telling me that he wanted to make love and I couldn't, I just couldn't—I didn't want to be bothered with him at all. He couldn't understand that 'cause he was a man and I felt that he was the same and he just kept pushing me and pushing me and pushing me and—

THERAPIST: And of course you never really told him what happened until recently, so he didn't know.

MOTHER: But he did know in a way.

FATHER: I had an idea, but she never took—she would never say. I asked her several times.

MOTHER: I can always tell when another woman has been mutilated or violated. I can tell.

THERAPIST: Can you?

MOTHER: Yes I can.

THERAPIST: How can you tell, Lily?

MOTHER: 'Cause there's a sadness. Unless she has really worked it out of her system and I don't think that you ever really work that out of your system, I really don't. There's a—there's a—there's somewhat of a—not a coldness, but a sadness. A morbidity somewhat—to some extent.

THERAPIST: Oh, I think things stay with you. I think that's true, but you see, I think the piece that has stayed with you, that gets into the marriage is that—your fear of being overpowered and the conflict around that and that you want a powerful man. You really do. So on the one hand you really do try to encourage him and—umm—help him in every way that you can to really achieve in the world and to do—but you are afraid of being overpowered. So that's how it gets into—that's the basic way it gets into the marriage. That's the conflict. That's the dilemma. It gets into your life in other ways.

Comments: The therapist uses the mother's information to maintain the therapeutic reality that has been previously constructed.

MOTHER: I don't know, I've been in therapy before and it just seems like it pops up—

THERAPIST: Okay, but the guys weren't there with you.

Comments: Following the mother's report that her previous therapy kept things the same, the therapist addresses how a change has already occurred—this therapy includes the whole family.

MOTHER: No.

THERAPIST: You were doing it all yourself and you can't do this job all by yourself, see? William has to help you with it.

FATHER: There's one thing I—there's one thing I want to tell you about. See, she has a phobia about something that has to be resolved because I tell her either she's going to resolve it or she has to put it to sleep. Put it on the shelf and forget about it. Somewhere in her childhood somebody must have played a dirty joke on her or something, but she has—well, it's not normal—a phobia about vampires. You know? Like she can't even—if a picture—if they're showing a presentation of a picture it will wreck her—believe me, she goes through a trip. You know? And we don't turn it on. If we know there's going to be an advertisement or if there is an advertisement in the newspaper it's like—umm—something—I'd like to get into that.

Comments: More meaningful noise is presented.

THERAPIST: Particularly vampires.

FATHER: Just—that's it, that's the only thing. Just that. And it's been worrying her for a long time.

THERAPIST: And yet she bought Benji a T-shirt that says "Beast."

FATHER: That's just one particular one, though. There's got to be something to that.

THERAPIST: Well, I would guess that that's probably connected with the same image of being overpowered by what must have seemed to you like a frightening beast. No?

Comments: Even the fascinating metaphors about the mother's vampire phobia and the beast T-shirt she bought Benji are utilized by the therapist as further evidence for maintaining the therapeutic reality.

MOTHER: I don't know, but I don't like to talk about that subject. He's right about that. I can't deal with that. I really can't.

THERAPIST: Why do you think you didn't tell your mother? A little girl, eleven years old. That you kept that secret and didn't—

MOTHER: She would have probably told me that—umm—

FATHER: Say it.

MOTHER: She probably—well, she might have told me that I was dirty or that—umm—she didn't believe me or she might even have told me that it was my fault.

THERAPIST: She might have blamed you.

FATHER: That's the kind of relationship they had anyway. At that particular stage—

MOTHER: 'Cause he had told me that she wouldn't believe me anyway. She wouldn't take my word over his. 'Cause I had told him if he didn't stop that I was going to tell my mother. And he had told me, "She would never believe you anyway."

FATHER: That was true.

THERAPIST: Did he stop?

MOTHER: Well, at some point he did, yeah.

THERAPIST: But it went on for a while.

MOTHER: Um-hum.

THERAPIST: Um-hum.

MOTHER: And—umm—

THERAPIST: When you told William about it, what kind of response did you get? When you really told him what had actually happened.

MOTHER: He told me that it didn't matter and that it wasn't my fault and that I was a better person—you know—God meant for it to happen and that he said that he was going to call my mother and tell my mother. I begged him not to, but then when he used to get drunk he used to throw it up in my face and tell me that, "Well, I'm going to call her and tell her." You know—then one time he even called me a whore and that really broke me down 'cause he knew how I felt about that, but this is when he was drinking. He wouldn't have done that if he wasn't drinking, and it kind of stayed with me. It kind of scarred me. That's a subject that I don't get into. That's like— that's like—that's very sacred to me.

THERAPIST: Yes. I would think so.

MOTHER: 'Cause I can'—I can't talk about it, really. It's difficult. Very difficult for me to. Takes a lot of—taking a lot of courage for me right now to talk about it in an adult way without being emotional and acting like a foolish child.

THERAPIST: Well, it's an emotional issue.

FATHER: There's a lot of reasons why I don't particularly care for her mother, but she assumes that it's just dislike for certain reasons. See I was—I was there during the—we've been together for almost eighteen, seventeen years from child—from when we met, sixteen years old, and I saw a lot of things and I saw how she treated her and I just couldn't understand why she has so much affection for this woman who didn't actually care that much about her and it was—I—I just couldn't conceive why a person would take so much abuse without breaking off, but then she did later on. She went to her grandmother's and then she—

MOTHER: I moved out.

FATHER: —moved out.

THERAPIST: You moved out.

MOTHER: 'Cause my grandmother had a feeling that something was wrong, but she couldn't prove anything cause I never said anything.

THERAPIST: You never said anything to grandmother either. Nobody.

MOTHER: He did. He broke my word. I made him promise not to tell anybody and he told my grandmother.

FATHER: I was drinking, though.

MOTHER: He was drinking and he—and he—he—

THERAPIST: The wonderful thing about drink is that it gives you permission to say all kind of things—

Comments: The therapist hints a possible positive consequence of the father's drinking.

FATHER: Anything you want to say. No, I—I—I—

MOTHER: He had no right to do that. That really affected me when he did that. He did that recently. He only did that a couple of months ago. And that really affected me emotionally 'cause I felt like I was in a glass house and everybody was looking at my soul now, and I had told that in confidence and I had told him never to tell it to anybody else and he did.

FATHER: I did it for a reason, though. 'Cause it did— You've been holding this thing in by yourself. I know—

MOTHER: That's my business. It happened to me— It's none of your concern.

FATHER: I know it's no good for you to carry—anybody to carry a secret around by themselves without sharing it. Now it's— now it's just not—it's not a secret. It can't be as great a magnitude as it was before because people are telling you, Lily, it wasn't your fault.

MOTHER: People haven't told me anything because I've never discussed it with my grandmother.

THERAPIST: Does Grandma ever mention it to you?

MOTHER: She acts like she doesn't know about it.

THERAPIST: She acts like she doesn't know about it.

FATHER: Well, I swore her to secrecy.

MOTHER: And knowing her with her big mouth she might have told the whole family.

THERAPIST: William told you that he told your grand-mother?

FATHER: Yup.

THERAPIST: You told her. Um-hum.

FATHER: I told her.

MOTHER: Yeah. He got drunk one night and told me that he told her.

FATHER: I don't think I was drunk when I told you that.

MOTHER: You was drinking, William, and that's why I was so upset because I had told you if you was sober you would have never done that.

FATHER: Maybe I was. Maybe I was.

THERAPIST: Okay.

FATHER: But my intentions were good.

THERAPIST: Of course what—we're about here and the relationship that counts is the one between the two of you. Whatever there is or was in the past, the only importance of it is how it affects your life together. Yours and the children's. Right? So I'm not asking you these questions because I'm nosy or curious about your past—

Comments: The therapist pushes the political frame of their present relationship to the foreground.

FATHER: I understand.

THERAPIST: —I only want to know how it affects your present. And I had that feeling and now too that I would be concerned, you see, if you become too strong, too fast.

FATHER: I sensed it. I sensed it and I had a little—I had a little resentment because I—she—I guess she—it really wraps up into women altogether—you know? How they've always been dominant in my life and the last thing I wanted was to be dominated by another female. I guess that's truly what it was and the stronger I got, I could sense that she felt uneasy, so I would attack that point. I was a child, really, and a devilish little brat and I would attack that point to see a reaction, 'cause I always liked to see a reaction.

THERAPIST: Yeah, but you see, you're so sensitive to her that without even knowing it you know when you're getting too strong and you're scaring her.

FATHER: Yeah. I do.

THERAPIST: So then I don't know how you would get yourself down again. Maybe by drinking or in some way sort of reassure her that she doesn't have to be afraid of you.

Comments: A positive social consequence of his drinking is now clearly defined.

FATHER: I guess it's all entwined together. I would say so.

THERAPIST: See, and then there's the other piece of it for you. You know—like we talked about—you know—how complicated it is. That what you get reactive to is when you feel you're being bossed around by her.

FATHER: Oh, yeah.

THERAPIST: Or anybody, or any woman for that matter. 'Cause—I mean—that's been a story—any woman, then you have to do the opposite.

FATHER: Anybody. I guess it really comes down to anybody. That's why I never— Corporate structure just wasn't for me because that's regimentation and I just never—I don't conform. I like doing my thing, you know. So I'd rather go into business for myself because I'm a very creative person. Anytime somebody tells me to do it, even now, in—in work, I have a resentment, you know? Because—I don't know why.

THERAPIST: Oh yeah, we do know why. Right?

FATHER: Yeah, we do know why. (*Laughing*) Sure, I know why.

THERAPIST: So we know why. See?

FATHER: Definitely.

THERAPIST: So we also know that the dilemma is that you come here and you want some help from me.

FATHER: Yes, ma'am.

THERAPIST: Right. I know that. I really do know that. That you sincerely want some help from me, but on the other hand the dilemma is that if I help you then you're going to feel like you're not helping yourself, so sometimes you're going to come and sometimes you're going to show me that you don't need me so much and you won't come. So, that's okay too.

Comments: The therapist broadens her description of the therapeutic reality to encompass the political organization of therapy.

FATHER: I'll tell you, I've been feeling good about things lately. And I haven't felt good—I can't remember how long it's been. I've always been depressed my entire life 'cause when I was a child I was an only child. My grandparents were raised—my grandmother and my aunt—the gap was so tremendous—there was no communication that I could deal with so I was depressed. I drank at the age of thirteen right on up until now so I've really never been happy. But now, I'm finally starting to put things together. Why I've been feeling the way I've been feeling—the way I felt. How I have to change in order not to do the things that I did in the past and a calm is really settling in and I'm not as hyper as I was. I don't need that drink. I find a middle that's really good. It's a good feeling and I'm feeling happy about that.

THERAPIST: Okay. Well, that's good, I'm very glad to hear that, but I just want to tell you that if you begin to get worried, concerned that he's getting a little bit too powerful and you begin to feel a little overpowered by him, the best thing you can do is to begin to nag him about something because he's very reactive to that. That's how you can get him back. That's how you can get him down. (*Laughing*)

> *Comments:* The therapist acknowledges both change and stability and prescribes that they use their "problematic" pattern of interaction as a resource—a means of preventing them from changing too fast.

FATHER: Sure. Brings me right down. She knows it. She knows it too. She says, "I'm the only one that can push your button. Nobody else can."

THERAPIST: That's the button.

FATHER: That's the button.

THERAPIST: If you want to know what the button is, that's the button. That will get things right back to where they were and you won't have to be so scared of him. Right?

FATHER: She—that's—that's a fact.

THERAPIST: Well, that's the way, but you know there are so many things we know without knowing that we know them.

> *Comments:* This is meaningful noise about meaningful noise.

FATHER: Yeah.

THERAPIST: You don't know you know them, but you know them and you know just how to keep each other at a certain level of functioning, which keeps things sort of the same.

FATHER: That's very true.

MOTHER: I'll tell you one thing I've noticed, Mrs. Silverstein. Since he's been here, I've noticed in him some sort of hope. He's got hope. Before he had a doomed attitude. But he seems to be—he feels like there's hope for him now. That's one thing I haven't said since he's been here.

THERAPIST: Okay. But you just don't want to move it too fast—

Comments: Throughout the sessions, the therapist has addressed the complementarity of change and stability by commenting on the rate of change. If the family announces a change, the therapist expresses her concern that it may be too fast. If the family announces that no progress (or a reversal) has occurred, the therapist praises their wisdom for not changing too quickly. As was mentioned earlier, both these messages have the effect of framing (and prescribing) the family as changing with a respect for stability.

MOTHER: See, that's what I'm afraid of.

THERAPIST: —'cause there's hope for him as long as he doesn't scare you. Okay?

MOTHER: Oh, that's true.

THERAPIST: 'Cause whatever hope there is for him is wound up with how it works with you so, it's a—you know, it's a balance between the two of you. We want to just—so just—you know— It will take some time and—

MOTHER: You think I'll ever get over my phobias that I have? I have those—I think that could have some—

THERAPIST: I think you're always going to be a little bit nervous about certain things, okay? But I think you'll manage them and the important thing again is to keep it out of the relationship between the two of you and your relationship with the children.

MOTHER: It's kind of hard.

THERAPIST: Of course it's hard. It's very hard.

MOTHER: Because it's a part of me.

THERAPIST: Absolutely, but you have to keep reminding yourself that this is a different man.

The therapist and family subsequently scheduled an appointment for another session. Several days before that meeting, the husband called and said that things were going well: he was attending AA meetings and was still enrolled in night school. In addition, he stated that they could not attend the next session.

The therapist responded that she respected their decision and that she felt that, since things had moved too fast, it was a good idea to slow things down a bit. He became annoyed with this suggestion and argued that he had no intention of slowing down. Subsequently, he requested no further appointments.

The therapist called the family four months later and spoke with the older son. He stated, "Dad has not been drinking; he has been coming to watch me play football; I have joined a small jazz band [he plays the drums] and am very busy." In addition, he said that his parents were not fighting very much since "everybody is too busy with their own thing." The therapist sent her regards to his parents and he promised to tell them she had called.

In conclusion, Olga Silverstein's strategy for organizing systemic family therapy can be summarized as using complementarities to construct and manage a therapeutic reality. The most fundamental complementarity discussed was that of semantics and politics. If the family presented a semantic frame, Silverstein subsequently exposed its political consequences. On the other hand, any family political frame was countered by some semantic frame of meaning.

The construction of complementarities also occurred within semantic and political frames. For instance, if the family indicated a political request for change, Silverstein would address the complementary side of stability or vice versa. On the side of semantics, defining the problem behavior of one family member was linked to defining the helping behavior of another family member. This, in turn, led to a view that demonstrated the shifting roles of this complementarity.

As we saw, the construction of semantic and political frames, the basic building blocks of systemic family therapy, took place largely in the first session. The next stage of therapy involved connecting these communicational frames in a way that constructed a useful therapeutic foundation. The interactional consequences of this therapeutic foundation were articulated to the family at the end of Session 2 and provided a structure for constructing higher-order complementarities throughout the latter two sessions. Namely, all family communication was demonstrated as fitting logically into a systemic therapeutic reality. In this way the family's communication—whether historical information, problem behavior, or future speculation—was demonstrated as not only making sense but as acknowledging that the family must continue changing with a respect for stability.

Having constructed and maintained such a therapeutic reality, the therapeutic sessions could be terminated, although the therapy would not necessarily finish. In other words, the family took the therapeutic reality with them—whatever happens in the future will always be contextualized by the therapeutic reality that was constructed in these four sessions. Should the family arrange to see the therapist again, what would probably occur is that the therapist would transform their communication into further refinement and maintenance of the original therapeutic reality. The art of systemic family therapy, as practiced by Olga Silverstein, is thus no less and no more than the construction and maintenance of alternative family realities.

Afterword

The Thomas family initally came to Olga Silverstein with an experiential reality that centered around the father's drinking problem. They presented descriptions of other problems, but in their world view these were all consequences of the father's drinking behavior. After four sessions with Silverstein their experiential reality had become transformed. The father's drinking had become contextualized as making sense from the perspective of this alternative therapeutic reality. For instance, the therapy sessions built the view that his drinking was a means of maintaining loyalty to black men, including his own father. In addition, his drinking behavior provided a way of calibrating his wife's fear of being overwhelmed by a strong man which, in turn, helped her to be closer to her first son as well as to rebel against her mother. And as the last session suggested, his drinking problem also provided a way of getting his wife into therapy.

The therapeutic reality constructed by Silverstein and the Thomas family involved more than turning their view of the father's drinking upside down. All descriptions of problem behavior were depicted as representing half of a more encompassing complementarity involving the action of another person. For instance, the mother's nagging at her husband was depicted as a way of protecting him from disappointments. It was also described as a way of protecting her from being overwhelmed by his becoming too strong. The construction of these complementarities enabled the family's reality to shift from a focus on the politics and meaning of simple action to the higher-order realities of social interaction and relationship ecology.

Beginning with the father's drinking, the therapeutic reality quickly moved to a political level that examined the sequential organization of social behavior that often organized his drinking. This sequence involved the father's withdrawal, the mother's subsequent efforts to prod him, followed by a marital argument and the father's increased drinking. This interactional sequence was in turn seen as organized by the more encompassing patterns of social choreography that involved the participation of their two sons and other family members, particularly the grandmother. The next level of politics that the therapy addressed was the connection of other people who were trying to help them, including Silverstein's involvement as their therapist. And finally, all of these political frames were seen as circumscribed by the political patterns enacted by their families of origin—in the past and the present.

With the construction of a well-formed systemic therapeutic reality, Silverstein was able to point out the advantages and disadvantages of so-called "problem" behavior. In addition she was able to demonstrate how all their behavior was connected to the family system in such a way that change in one person would be countered by another family member so as to maintain relationship stability. This helped shift the focus from unilineal change of individuals to the complementary dance between change and stability across levels of simple action, interaction, and social ecology.

Olga Silverstein's involvement in this therapeutic reality included more than helping the family construct more adaptive frames of meaning. She actively participated in changing the sequential organization of their interaction and utilized her own relationship with family members as a lever for organizational change.

With respect to the major interventions developed in this case, recall that Session 1 included the therapist addressing the theme of "mothering." This theme was used to suggest that she continued to "mother" her husband but that she had changed from a "good mother" to an "angry mother." In terms of stability, change, and meaningful noise we have:

(Stability of mothering/Change in style of mothering)/
Meaningful noise of the theme of mothering

This intervention planted the seed that the therapy would move toward approaching patterns of social organization rather than an isolated focus on any particular individual. In addition, it provided the first example of how the therapist would respond to their communication in terms of complementarity. In this case, mother's report of change was countered by the therapist pointing out its relation to stability.

In the second session the therapeutic foundation was constructed in terms of the general themes of "expectations" and "disappointments." Stability, change, and meaningful noise were then addressed as follows:

(Stability of men's loyalty (disappointment)/
Change requested by women (expectations))/
Meaningful noise of family history and cultural myth

The women's high expectations for men were defined as leading the men to rebel against the women. This rebellion had the positive consequence of maintaining loyalty to black men (in terms of not being an "Uncle Tom"), but had the cost of disappointment since they must fail in order to rebel.

With this therapeutic foundation and intervention the therapeutic reality more solidly moved to the level of interaction rather than simple action. Consequently, the beginning of the third session included working on the interactional sequence that involved mother's mind reading of her husband's silence and the subsequent development of marital fighting and escalated drinking. In the third session, the therapist's main intervention even more clearly exposed the interactional structure of their situation. The therapist depicted how stability of their relationship was maintained by change of either individual.

Their relationship was defined as complementary, wherein they took turns enacting the roles of the strong and weak member. With this view, stability, change, and meaningful noise were addressed as follows:

(Stability of complementary relationship (strong/weak)/
Changing roles)/Meaningful noise of family descriptions

Here change in one spouse's role—whether as the identified patient or the identified helper—was depicted as maintaining their complementary relationship.

The therapist ended the third session by recycling the therapeutic intervention of Session 2 that defined their situation as a dilemma where the father's rebellion against the mother's expectations provided a means of maintaining family loyalty as well as a disappointing failure. The therapist, however, went a step further and began to define the mother's dilemma in this situation as having to do with her simultaneous desire and fear of strong men.

The final session more carefully spelled out the mother's side of the dilemma and underscored how her husband's problem provided a corrective solution of her fear of strong men. At this point the complementary connection between the husband and wife had been fully explicated. Each spouse had been depicted as having "problem behavior" that provided a "solution" for the other spouse. In addition, the final session connected their relationship to the political participation of other family members, particularly the triadic relations of the mother, the father, and the older son. The therapist's political participation in the social ecology was also utilized as a further means of maintaining the therapeutic reality.

The last session constructed a final intervention that put the family into a therapeutic double bind. Problems were generalized as the family's own resource for preventing them from changing too fast. Any report of a lack of change was therapeutically framed as an indication that the family was slowly and appropriately changing with a respect for stability. Any report of change was framed as an indication that the family should be cautious about changing too fast. The net effect of these therapeutic frames was that the family was caught in a reality where change prescribed stability and stability prescribed change. In terms of stability, change, and meaningful noise, we finally have:

(A report of change means that the family should pay more attention to stability/A report of stability means that the family should continue present rate of change that is respectful of stability)/ Meaningful noise of all family semantics and politics

The either/or polarities that initially threatened the family's survival were fully transformed into a complementary structure in which all the meaningful noise of family semantics and politics became connected in a dialectical fashion. In this dialectic the family had a more adaptive means of constructing its own unique development.

The family's reports of ongoing changes throughout the sessions and the therapist's follow-up call are indications that the therapy was successful. Evaluating the final success of a case, however, is as slippery a task as initially assessing the problem to work on. Some therapists, as is well known, believe that a series of psychological (and sociological) tests and diagnostic procedures must first be given in order to make an assessment of the problem (as well as of the outcomes). Systemic therapists are aware that such a ritual is itself an intervention and an incantation for constructing a particular form of therapeutic reality. Silverstein's approach is to accept the family's own choice of semantic frames and to view and utilize these frames as a way of approaching family politics.

This approach suggests a radically different epistemological understanding of what we regard as "problems" and "outcomes." For the systemic therapist there are no "real problems." Rather there are "constructed problems," that in turn have "constructed consequences." As a demonstration of this constructivist position, imagine asking a client about his or her problem. Independent of the client's particular response, imagine the therapist subsequently responding with the question, "Please, what is your *real* problem?" More than likely, the client will offer a different semantic frame. As a further step, consider the therapist then responding with the question, "As I now speak to your unconscious mind, what is your deepest and most basic problem?" Again it is likely that the client will construct an entirely different semantic definition of the problem. The question for an observer of this scenario is: "Which of the client's responses indicates the 'real' problem?"

Similarly, views of therapeutic outcomes are constructed. Asking a client what happened in therapy can always be followed by asking what really happened, and so on. In this way, clients and therapists construct the meanings and subsequent political consequences of their situation. As was indicated, Silverstein's approach to systemic therapy sidesteps these naive ontological traps by fully accepting and utilizing the client's own choice of semantics. From her domain of observation, however, she organizes her responses with a view of complementarity. This view suggests, for example, that the question, "Has the family changed?," is always incomplete. The more systemic question is, "How is the family stabilizing and changing?" Similarly, in the beginning of therapy, she is interested in knowing about more than the family's problem. She is interested in knowing about their problems and their solutions, as well as the disadvantages and advantages accompanying each.

In sum, a systemic view of complementarity enables all responses of the family to be utilized in a generative fashion. Knowing that any particular response can be seen as a description about part of a more encompassing pattern enables the therapist to address the implied parts. In this way therapeutic dialogue is generated. As we indicated in the theoretical introduction, systemic therapy has nothing to do with medicine—it is within the domain of rhetoric and dialogue. Rather than offering cures and solutions, an alternative reality is built which transforms the meaning and politics of the people who are part of it, including family members and therapists.

References

Bateson, G. (1979). *Mind and nature: A necessary unity.* New York: E. P. Dutton.

Haley, J. (1976). *Problem-solving therapy.* San Francisco: Jossey-Bass.

Keeney, B. (1983). *Aesthetics of change.* New York: Guilford Press.

Keeney, B., & Ross, J. (1985). *Mind in therapy: Constructing systemic family therapies.* New York: Basic Books.

Papp, P. (1983). *The process of change.* New York: Guilford Press.

Selvini-Palazzoli, M., Cecchin, G., Prata, G., & Boscolo, L. (1978). *Paradox and counterparadox.* New York: Jason Aronson.

Snyder, G. (1979). Poetry, Community and Climax. *Field, 20,* 21–36.

Szasz, T. (1978). *The myth of psychotherapy.* New York: Anchor Books.

Watzlawick, P., Weakland, J., & Fisch, R. (1974). *Change: Principles of problem formation and problem resolution.* New York: W. W. Norton.

Index